The Avocado Cookbook

Jill Graham

First published 1983 by
AH & AW REED PTY LTD
2 Aquatic Drive Frenchs Forest NSW 2086
68 Kingsford-Smith Street Wellington 3 NZ

This edition distributed by Wattle Books 1983

National Library of Australia
Cataloguing-in-Publication Data
Graham, Jill.
The avocado cookbook.
Includes index.
ISBN 0 589 50375 8.
1. Cookery (Avocado). I. Title.
641.6'4653

Photography by Andrew Warn and Jill Graham
Designed by Robbylee Phelan
Set in Benguiat Medium by B&D Modgraphic Pty Ltd, Adelaide
Printed and bound by Dai Nippon Printing Co (Hong Kong) Ltd

Contents

Acknowledgements

Thank you to Mr Fred Chalker, horticulturist extraordinaire of the New South Wales Department of Agriculture and to members of the CSIRO Department of Food Research for their time and generous help.

And to Dr Vincent T. Flynn of Nambour, Queensland for his help with nutritional details.

Once again Andrew Warn has taken beautiful photographs of my food, and I sincerely thank him.

And a special thank you to my family and friends who were my 'guinea pigs'.

Jacket illustration
Orange and Avocado Compôte, page 78
A delicious combination of fruit marinated in a tangy liqueur.

Introduction

What can you do with an avocado? Use it to make hot or chilled soup, dips and pâtés, add it to pies and casseroles, bake it or turn it into ice-cream, cakes and desserts.

The avocado is the fruit of a tree, Persea americana, *a member of the laurel family which includes cinnamon, bay, sassafras and camphor. Native to Central America, the home of the Aztecs, the tree originally grew wild and archaeologists have found the remains of seeds dating back to 5000 BC. No one seems to know exactly when the spread of the wild avocado plants began but it was probably by tribal exchange for other food crops. It was being extensively cultivated in Central America by the time the Spanish conquistadors invaded the Aztec empire. From there the plants began to travel, to southern Spain in the early 1600s, then to the West Indies, in the early 1800s to California, Florida and Texas and gradually to Hawaii, the Philippines, Africa and the Canary Islands, Israel, parts of Asia and Australia. Like any other food taken from country to country avocados have had the flavour, culture and use of those countries imposed upon them, each one adding new ideas towards the enjoyment of this highly nutritious food.*

Continuing experiments with growing techniques and regions as well as cross breeding mean that avocados are available to us for most of the year, and it seems a pity to restrict ourselves to using this useful food in only one or two ways when it can turn up quite appropriately as a starter, main course, vegetable or dessert.

Guide to Weights and Measures

The metric weight and fluid measures throughout this book comply with the Australian Standard Metric Measures. A good set of scales is an asset in any kitchen and a graduated set of metric cups and spoons will be most helpful. These are readily available in hardware and department stores.

The Australian Standard measuring cup has a capacity of 250 millilitres (250 ml).

The Australian Standard tablespoon has a capacity of 20 millilitres (20 ml).

The Australian Standard teaspoon has a capacity of 5 millilitres (5 ml).

Important points

New Zealand, Canadian and American weights and measures are the same with the exception that the Australian Standard measuring tablespoon is larger than that of New Zealand, Canada and America, having a capacity of 20 ml compared to 15 ml in New Zealand and North America. For accuracy, where a recipe specifies 1 tablespoon use 4 teaspoonsful (or 4×5 ml measuring spoons) in New Zealand and North America.

It is also important to note that the New Zealand and Australian imperial pint has a capacity of 20 fl oz whereas the American and Canadian pint has a capacity of 16 fl oz.

All spoon measurements are level spoonsful.

All flour mentioned is plain flour unless otherwise stated.

Note For successful cooking use either one or other of the measuring systems—all metric or all imperial—do not use a mixture of the two. The metric yield of cup or weighed measures is about 10 per cent greater than that of imperial but the proportions of either system are the same within each one.

Metric conversion

The conversion represented by this table is sufficiently accurate for cooking purposes: the precise conversion would be 28.3 grams to 1 imperial ounce.

METRIC dry measures (grams)	**IMPERIAL** dry measures (ounces)
15 g	½ oz
30 g	1 oz
60 g	2 oz
90 g	3 oz
125 g	4 oz (¼ lb)
185 g	6 oz
250 g	8 oz (½ lb)
375 g	12 oz (¾ lb)
500 g (0.5 kg)	16 oz (1 lb)
750 g	24 oz (1½ lb)
1000 g (1 kg)	32 oz (2 lb)
1500 g (1.5 kg)	3 lb
2000 g (2 kg)	4 lb

METRIC liquid measures (millilitres)	**CUPS**	**IMPERIAL** liquid measures (fluid ounces)	
30 ml		1 fl oz	
60 ml	¼ cup	2 fl oz	
100 ml		3 fl oz	
125 ml	½ cup	4 fl oz	¼ pt US
150 ml		5 fl oz	¼ pt imperial
250 ml	1 cup	8 fl oz	½ pt US
	1¼ cups	10 fl oz	½ pt imperial
	1½ cups	12 fl oz	
	1¾ cups	14 fl oz	
500 ml	2 cups	16 fl oz	1 pt US
	2½ cups	20 fl oz	1 pt imperial
1 litre	4 cups	32 fl oz	

All about Avocados

Buying

There are few fruits less appetising than an underripe avocado so unless your greengrocer is reliable it is inadvisable to believe that the rock-like avocado you buy today will be perfect for eating tomorrow, or even the next day. It is better by far to buy unripe avocados and ripen them at home (see *Ripening Avocados* page 10). This way they avoid the pressures of market rough-and-tumble and the multiple pinches of prospective customers.

The size of the avocado you choose depends upon the recipe, the season, and the number of people to be served. Very tiny avocados with a high percentage of stone and peel are really poor value compared with one large fruit which will adequately serve four people.

Overripe avocados are usually bruised but very cheap. The bruised parts can be removed and the rest used for recipes that call for mashed or puréed avocado, dips and pâtés. They should be used on the day of purchase.

Avocado sizes

In some recipes I have indicated the avocado size, small, medium, etc. To clarify what I mean, here is a guide. Weigh a few, or have a few weighed by the greengrocer, and you will soon be able to tell at a glance how much an avocado weighs. Very small and poor value, 100 g or under; small 200 g; medium 300 g; large 400 g; very large 500–600 g.

Where a recipe does not give a specific avocado size then the end result is unaffected by the amount of avocado you use.

Cocktail avocados

Seedless cocktail avocados, cukes, are biological offcuts but nevertheless make fine eating. Several may be used where a recipe calls for one large avocado, or use them peeled and sliced or whole, in salads or as a garnish.

Storage

Do not store unripe avocados in the refrigerator. Avocados dislike frost and will soon blacken and deteriorate.

Ripe avocados may be stored in the vegetable crisper of a refrigerator and 'held' for 5 or 6 days.

Once cut, avocados should not be exposed to air for longer than necessary before being served or added to a recipe because the flesh darkens with oxidation. To overcome this problem brush the cut surface of the fruit with cold water or citrus juice. Store unused avocado halves in the refrigerator. Leave the stone in place and cover closely with plastic wrap. They will remain in good condition for 2 to 3 days.

Deep freezing

Whole, unpeeled avocados will blacken when frozen but avocado purée freezes well for 2 to 3 months.

To each cup of avocado purée add 3 teaspoons lemon juice or ¼ cup castor sugar. Blend thoroughly, pack into a suitable container and cover the purée closely with a disc of freezer film. Leave about 1 cm of headspace for each cup of purée, seal, label and date the container before freezing.

Preparation

Using a stainless steel or silver knife to cut avocados will avoid discoloration of the fruit. Slice into the fruit lengthways, cutting to the centre stone and using it as a firming guide to go round. Gently lever the halves apart with the knife, or turn the halves in opposite directions until they separate. Strike the stone with the sharp edge of the knife and twist free.

If you are going to use the shells, scoop out the flesh with a spoon or melon ball cutter. Brush the fruit with a little citrus juice or cold water to prevent discoloration.

Peeled avocados are very slippery. To slice the fruit, peel the skin away and place the avocado, cut side down, on a board. Cut thick or thin slices lengthways or crossways as you wish, and both ways for cubes.

Do not discard the darkest green layer of the avocado—it lies close to the skin and sometimes comes away with the peel. This has the most delicate flavour and can be used in the dressing or sauce of the recipe.

How to ripen avocados in a hurry

The whole ripening process can be accelerated by putting the avocado into a paper (not plastic) bag with a ripe banana or apple for company. Fold the top of the bag over a couple of times and keep it in a drawer or dark cupboard for a day or so. The ripening is probably hastened by the natural ethylene gas from the companion fruit. This is the gas used commercially for ripening other fruits.

Nutritional values

Weight for weight avocados are better all round nourishment than any other fruit. They have the highest protein content of all and only bananas have more fibre. Particularly abundant in vitamin E, avocados contain ten other vitamins, eight minerals and pectin. While the oil content is second only to that of olives, seventy-five per cent of the fats are polyunsaturated and they contain absolutely no cholesterol. They are also very low in carbohydrates.

However, although avocados have a low sugar content they do contain a sugar called mannoheptulose which very quickly elevates blood sugar levels. This is very good for people with low blood sugars and those needing a quick boost, but makes them unsuitable for inclusion in a diabetic diet.

Avocado curiosities

If conversation fails and all else lags you can always throw in some of these items for good measure.

Ahuacatl, the Nahuactl word for avocado was converted to *abocado*, meaning advocate by the Spaniards, and the French call the fruit *avocat* still.

Avocados are not pears but have been known as the alligator pear, clearly because of the gnarled skin of some varieties; as the Spanish pear, since it was the Spanish who first transplanted the trees inter-continentally; and as the butter pear, probably because of their colour and buttery texture. A host of other buttery names existed during the time of sailing ships—midshipman's, subaltern's and poor man's butter. Not difficult to imagine how those names came about—early sailors would have relished the avocado after weeks at sea on a limited diet.

Avocado purée may aid if applied to sunburn. I have not tried it but avocados do have a high vitamin E content so it is feasible.

If you have no intention of moving in a hurry an avocado seed planted in your garden may bear fruit in seven years.

And finally a Mexican myth holds that if you carve the seed of an avocado into the shape of a girl or boy it will determine the sex of an unborn child.

Avocado ideas

This book is mainly concerned with the inclusion of avocados in cooked recipes. There are of course many uses for uncooked avocados and here are a few suggestions.

At their simplest, mashed and spread on toast with a little seasoning and lemon juice they make an excellent breakfast.

Sliced avocados served with a hot chocolate sauce make a delicious and unusual dessert.

To a mashed avocado on toast or bread you can instantly create canapés or open sandwiches by adding crisply cooked bacon, grated cheese, smoked salmon, caviar or chopped prawns. Shredded lettuce and chopped shallots are good together, as are chopped apple and anchovies. The combinations are endless.

One large avocado is enough to spread generously onto six slices of bread or toast, on six open sandwiches or 24 canapés.

If you want to prepare sandwiches or titbits for a party, mash the avocado with a little lemon or lime juice and it will not discolour for many hours.

Dips, Hors d'oeuvres and Pâtés

The whole area of dips, hors d'oeuvres and pâtés is tricky. They are so tempting and so easy to eat with a pre-dinner drink that we run the risk of taking the edge from appetites instead of stimulating them. Finger food made with avocados is light, less likely to ruin your appetite or your waistline, or have a devastating effect on your dinner.

PRAWN AND AVOCADO DIP

250 g peeled cooked prawns (approx. 500 g unpeeled weight)
1 clove garlic, crushed
1 small avocado, peeled, stoned and sliced
2–3 tablespoons lemon juice
salt
black pepper
paprika
plain crackers or corn chips for serving

Reduce the prawns to a coarse paste in a food processor or blender. Add the garlic and avocado and blend well. Season to taste with lemon juice, salt and pepper. Pile into a dish and chill. Sprinkle with paprika before serving.

Makes 1½ cups

SMOKY BLENDER DIP

75 g smoked eel, skinned and boned
5 sprigs parsley, coarsely chopped
3 shallots, white and some green parts, chopped
1 small avocado, peeled and stoned
2 tablespoons heavy sour cream
1½–2 tablespoons lemon juice
salt
black pepper
1 teaspoon prepared horseradish
crisp toast or plain crackers for serving

This dip does not discolour readily so can be prepared well in advance.

Blend the eel for a few seconds until crumbly. Add the parsley, shallots, avocado and sour cream, blend until smooth. Add lemon juice, salt, pepper and horseradish to taste. (The grated, rather than creamed, horseradish is the best one to use here.) Pile the dip onto a dish, cover and leave at room temperature for 30 minutes to allow the flavour to develop. Chill before serving with the toast or crackers.

Serves 4–6

GUACAMOLE

There is a widespread belief that if you bury an avocado stone in the pulp it will prevent discoloration of the fruit. Unfortunately there is little foundation for this, no inherent magic in the stones, and the whole idea has probably derived from the Mexican Indian habit of laying the seeds over the surface of prepared guacamole. These act as an inhibitor of air, certainly, but less romantically, plastic wrap is far more efficient.

In Mexico guacamole is served with practically everything as a sauce for fish and poultry; as a spread, or dip, with tortillas or corn chips, and as a salad mounded into crisp cups of lettuce.

The Traditional Guacamole is quite different to the Californian Guacamole and I have included a version of each one. The first needs to be prepared and served within a short time because it will discolour. The second has a lighter consistency, and is more of a dip in texture. It can be prepared well ahead of time, even overnight. Covered, it can be abandoned in the refrigerator until ready to serve.

And as a final word I warn you that in Mexico guacamole is regarded as an aphrodisiac!

Traditional Guacamole

1 large avocado, peeled and stoned and mashed
1 small tomato, peeled and finely chopped
½ small onion, finely chopped
2 or more hot fresh or canned chillies, seeded and finely chopped
1 tablespoon chopped fresh coriander
salt
corn chips for serving

This is the gaucamole of Mexico. The recipe contains no citrus juice and, unlike the Californian Guacamole, (page 14) it will discolour, if not as you watch it then certainly within a couple of hours. However, it does take only a few minutes to prepare and the flavour is superb.

Blend the avocado, tomato and onion with the chillies. Add the coriander and season to taste with salt. Cover the guacamole closely with plastic wrap and chill for 15 minutes before serving with the crisp chips.

Makes 1¼ cups

Californian Guacamole

1 large avocado, peeled and stoned
1 tablespoon lemon juice
1 small onion, very finely chopped
1 small ripe tomato, peeled, seeded and chopped
2 or more hot green chillies, seeded and chopped
½ clove garlic, crushed
½–1 teaspoon Worcestershire sauce
1 tablespoon mayonnaise
pinch cayenne pepper
pinch ground coriander
salt
paprika
corn chips or crackers for serving

This is very useful as a dip, or a filling for hard-boiled eggs, tiny tomatoes or small choux pastry puffs.

Mash the avocado with a fork. Add the lemon juice and blend through the pulp. Add the onion, tomato, chillies and garlic. Add Worcestershire sauce to taste, the mayonnaise and spices. Season with salt, cover with plastic wrap and refrigerate for at least 1 hour. Sprinkle the guacamole generously with paprika before serving with corn chips or plain crackers.

Makes 1¼ cups

AVOCADO CACIK

1 cucumber, peeled, seeded and finely chopped
salt
½ cup heavy sour cream, whipped
1 medium-sized avocado, peeled, stoned and puréed
1 teaspoon lemon juice
1½ tablespoons finely chopped fresh mint
white pepper
paprika
extra mint leaves
plain crackers or crusty bread for serving

An uncomplicated dip, especially good for a hot summer day. Light and tangy, it will not sap your appetite.

Put the chopped cucumber into a colander, sprinkle with salt and leave to drain for 30 minutes. Pat the cucumber dry with paper towels and combine with the sour cream, avocado and lemon juice. Add the mint and season to taste with pepper and more salt if necessary. Turn the dip onto a serving dish. Sprinkle with paprika and swirl it lightly over the surface with a fork. Garnish with crisp mint leaves and chill before serving with unflavoured crackers or bread.

Makes 1¼ cups

PIQUANT AVOCADO PUFFS

1 quantity savoury Choux Pastry (page 85)
1 egg, lightly beaten
3 tablespoons cream cheese
1 avocado, peeled, stoned and mashed
3–4 teaspoons lemon juice
3–4 teaspoons prepared horseradish
salt
black pepper

Prepare the pastry and allow to become completely cool at room temperature (do not refrigerate before using). Preheat the oven to 200°C and line baking trays with non-stick paper or lightly oiled greaseproof paper. Using a plain 1 cm nozzle, fill a piping bag with the cold choux. Have ready a pair of kitchen scissors and a basin of cold water. Pipe 2 cm blobs of the choux pastry onto the baking sheets. Cut the piped pastry from the icing tube with the wet scissors. Brush the pastry lightly with egg and bake for 15–17 minutes until well puffed and golden. Cool on racks before filling. Blend the cream cheese and avocado and add the remaining ingredients to taste. Split the puffs with a sharp knife and spoon the filling between the halves.

Makes 24

GALA SPRING ROLLS

2 tablespoons ghee or butter
2 medium-sized onions, chopped
1 stalk celery, thinly sliced
2 teaspoons coarsely grated root ginger
1 cup bean sprouts
140 g can pimientos, drained and diced
90 g slivered almonds
1 avocado, peeled, stoned and diced
salt
black pepper
20 spring roll wrappers
oil for frying
Chinese plum or soy sauce for serving

These rolls can be prepared well in advance and fried for a few seconds before serving.

Melt the ghee or butter in a large shallow pan. Sauté the onions and celery until lightly browned. Add the ginger, bean sprouts, pimientos, almonds and avocado. Stir over low heat until well blended. Season generously with salt and pepper and cool. Divide the cooled mixture between the spring roll wrappers, placing a spoonful on each corner and rolling as a parcel. Fry the rolls in hot oil until crisp and golden. Drain on absorbent paper and serve with one or both of the sauces.

Makes 20 rolls

AVOCADO STUFFED EGGS

6–8 hard-boiled eggs
1 small, or ½ large avocado, mashed
1½ tablespoons lemon juice
1 tablespoon ricotta cheese
2 teaspoons mayonnaise
3 shallots, very finely chopped
salt
cayenne pepper

Halve the eggs lengthways. Remove the yolks and blend with the avocado, lemon juice, cheese and mayonnaise. Add the shallots and season to taste. Pipe or spoon the avocado mixture into the white shells and chill for 30 minutes before serving lightly sprinkled with cayenne pepper.

Serves 4–6

BAGNA BREAD

1 French bread stick, halved lengthways
2 tablespoons soft butter
1 large avocado, peeled and stoned
3 teaspoons lemon juice
salt
black pepper
2 small tomatoes, chopped and seeded
60 g button mushrooms, chopped
55 g jar anchovies, drained and chopped
1 tablespoon capers, chopped
10 stoned green olives, sliced
2 hot chillies, seeded and very finely chopped
2 tablespoons chopped fresh basil or parsley

Preheat the oven to 200°C. Scoop the soft bread from the centre of the halves leaving 1.5 cm shells. Butter the inside of the shells. Crumb the bread in a blender or food processor, add half the avocado and the lemon juice, blend until smooth. Season to taste and spread into the shells. Dice the rest of the avocado, mix with the remaining ingredients. Fill the loaf with the mixture, press the two halves together and secure with bands of twisted foil. Bake the bread for 10 minutes. Turn the oven off and allow the bread to cool slowly. Serve in slices.

Serves 6

Gala Spring Rolls, page 15
Crisp spring rolls with a savoury avocado filling.

Overleaf
Sardine and Avocado Pâté, page 19
A very simple pâté with a subtle blend of flavours.

SARDINE AND AVOCADO PÂTÉ

60 g softened butter
1 teaspoon French mustard
2 cans sardines in oil
60 g cream cheese
1 medium-sized avocado, peeled, stoned and mashed
lemon juice
salt
black pepper
black olives and wholemeal toast for serving

Try to buy Portuguese sardines for they have the sweetest and best flavour.

Blend the butter and mustard until light and fluffy. Reserve 2 teaspoons of the sardine oil. Split the sardines and remove the bones; they lift out quite easily. Discard any tails. Add the sardines, cheese and avocado to the butter and beat well. Season to taste with lemon juice, salt and plenty of black pepper. Fill a mould or pile the pâté onto a dish and chill. Pour the sardine oil over the pâté and serve with olives and toast. This pâté may be served in lemon or tomato shells for a change, or turned into a rather nice dip simply by adding 1 stiffly beaten egg white to the mixture after the final chilling.

Serves 6

CHICKEN AVOCADO PÂTÉ

5 teaspoons gelatine
½ cup cold water
1 cup chicken stock, or use cubes
1 avocado
4 tablespoons ghee or butter
1 medium-sized onion, chopped
500 g chicken livers, skinned and trimmed
1 clove garlic, crushed
⅛ teaspoon cayenne pepper
½ teaspoon dried tarragon
2 tablespoons dry sherry
salt
black pepper
2 tablespoons sour cream

Sprinkle the gelatine over cold water and stir over low heat until dissolved. Strain the gelatine with the stock, stir well and spoon a thin layer over the base of a mould. Peel and stone the avocado. Cut ¼ into thin slices and arrange decoratively over the base of the mould. Cover with a thin layer of gelatine and refrigerate. Brush the rest of the avocado with cold water and reserve. Melt the ghee or butter in a shallow pan and sauté the onion until transparent. Add the chicken livers and cook for 5–6 minutes, turning occasionally. Add the garlic, cayenne, tarragon and sherry, stir well and simmer for 3 or 4 minutes. Mash the remaining avocado with a fork. Remove the livers from the heat and blend with the avocado until smooth. (Use a blender, food processor or fork.) Season generously to taste, blend in the sour cream and the rest of the gelatine mixture. Spoon the pâté into the mould, level the surface and refrigerate for 6 hours or overnight.

Serves 8

SMOKED TROUT AND AVOCADO BRANDADE

1 smoked trout, skinned and boned
1 small avocado, peeled and stoned
2 tablespoons lemon juice
1 tablespoon olive oil
1 tablespoon cream
¼ teaspoon castor sugar
salt
black pepper
watercress or coriander
4 tablespoons melted ghee
toast for serving

Pound smoked trout until crumbly (you can use a blender or food processor). Add the avocado, blend until smooth. Add 1½ tablespoons of the lemon juice, oil, cream and sugar. Mix thoroughly, season to taste with salt, pepper and more lemon juice if necessary. Pack into one mould, or individual ramekins. Place the watercress or coriander leaves on top of the pâté, coat lightly with ghee and chill before serving.

Serves 4–6

KIPPERED AVOCADO PÂTÉ

2 kippers, or 1 can kipper fillets, drained
1 avocado
2 tablespoons softened butter
90 g cottage cheese
2–3 tablespoons lemon juice
black pepper
thin slices lemon
toast for serving

If using whole kippers put them into a shallow dish, cover with boiling water and steep for 2 minutes. Drain and cool. Peel and stone the avocado, cut 2 thin slices from one half, brush lightly with cold water and set aside. Beat the butter and cheese together until smooth and creamy. Mash the remaining avocado and blend with the cheese mixture. Skin, bone and chop the cooled kippers, blend with the avocado mixture adding lemon juice and pepper to taste. Pile the pâté into a dish or individual moulds and chill. Cut the reserved avocado slices into tiny dice. Garnish the chilled pâté with thin slices of lemon and diced avocado.

Serves 4–6

AVOCADO CHEESE PÂTÉ

1¼ cups milk
1 small onion, halved
1 medium-sized carrot, sliced
1 small stalk celery, sliced
4 peppercorns
2 cloves
1 bay leaf
1½ tablespoons butter
1½ tablespoons flour
salt
white pepper
6 sprigs watercress, leaves and stems separated
1 medium-sized avocado
2 tablespoons mayonnaise
1–2 tablespoons lemon juice
2 small cloves garlic, crushed
125 g blue vein cheese, crumbled
cayenne pepper
toast for serving

This pâté is also very good served in tiny scooped-out tomatoes as a party savoury.

Put the milk into a pan with the vegetables, peppercorns, cloves and bay leaf. Bring almost to boiling point then simmer, with the pan half covered, for 10 minutes. Strain the milk and discard the flavouring ingredients. Melt the butter in a heavy pan, stir in the flour to form a smooth paste (roux). Add some of the milk and boil briefly with the roux, remove from the heat and beat together until smooth. Repeat until all the milk has been added and a heavy sauce is formed. Season to taste, cover the surface of the sauce closely with plastic film and cool to handheat. Chop the watercress stems finely and set aside. Peel and stone the avocado, brush one half with cold water and reserve. Mash the other half with a fork and fold into the cool sauce with the mayonnaise, 1 tablespoon lemon juice, garlic and the chopped watercress stems. Dice the remaining avocado, fold into the mixture with the cheese and adjust the seasoning, adding more lemon juice if necessary. Spoon the pâté into 1 large or 6 individual moulds. Fork the tops level and chill. Serve the pâté lightly dusted with cayenne and garnished with the watercress leaves.

Serves 6

POTTED AVOCADO CHEESE

185 g matured Cheddar cheese, coarsely grated
60 g butter, at room temperature
1 medium-sized avocado, peeled and stoned
2 teaspoons lemon juice
pinch ground mace
coarsely ground pepper
salt
parsley sprigs to garnish
toast or crackers for serving

Blend the cheese with the softened butter. Mash the avocado with the lemon juice, add to the cheese butter and mix lightly together. Season to taste with mace, plenty of pepper (crushed, dried green peppercorns are best, or use black pepper), and salt if needed. Divide the mixture between 6 small ramekins and pack firmly. Fork the tops level or use the back of a small, hot spoon to smooth the surface. Press a tiny parsley sprig on top and chill before serving with plain crisp toast or crackers.

Serves 6

Soups

Warming in winter and delectably refreshing in summer, homemade soup is a delicious overture to any meal, or for a light lunch add a salad or a sandwich and the meal is complete.

Soup made with avocados, whether they comprise the main ingredient or a glamorous garnish, is luxury at very little cost.

The main thing to remember is that hot soup should be very hot and cold soup really chilled.

SIMPLE AVOCADO SOUP

2 small avocados
lemon juice
6 cups hot chicken stock
3 tablespoons cream
salt
white pepper

Halve and stone the avocados, brush one half with cold water and reserve. Peel the remaining avocados, chop roughly and blend, until smooth, with 3 teaspoons of lemon juice. Stir the avocado purée into the simmering stock. Add the cream and season to taste. Heat the soup without boiling for about 2 minutes. Peel and slice the reserved avocado thinly and add to the soup just before serving.

Serves 6–8

FRESH MUSHROOM AND AVOCADO SOUP

2 teaspoons butter
185 g white button mushrooms, thinly sliced
4 cups chicken stock, or use cubes
2 egg yolks
1½ tablespoons cream
salt
pepper
lemon juice
1 small avocado

Melt the butter in a saucepan set over low heat. Add the mushrooms, stir with the butter and simmer for 5 minutes. Add the stock, bring to the boil then simmer very gently for 10 minutes. Blend the egg yolks and cream in a basin, add 2 tablespoons of the soup and mix well. Whisk the egg mixture into the soup which must not boil after this point. Season to taste with salt, pepper and lemon juice. Peel, stone and slice the avocado thinly. Add to the soup and heat through for 2–3 minutes before serving.

Serves 4–6

CHILLED AVOCADO SOUP

2 medium-sized avocados, peeled and stoned
2–3 tablespoons lemon juice
2½ cups chilled chicken stock
1 cup cream
salt
white pepper
2 tablespoons finely chopped chives

Brush one quarter of one avocado with water and reserve. Purée the avocados in a food processor or blender, or mash with a fork and sieve. Gradually blend the purée with 2 tablespoons of the lemon juice. Add the stock and cream and season to taste, adding more of the lemon juice if liked. Season the soup fairly generously as cold food loses some flavour. Chill the soup before serving garnished with the chopped avocado and chives.

Serves 6

AVOCADO SOUP AILLARDE

2 large avocados, peeled and stoned
3 teaspoons lemon juice
2 cups cool chicken stock, or use cubes
pinch ground cumin
1 clove garlic, crushed
½ cup milk
¾ cup cream
salt
white pepper
finely chopped chives to garnish

A soup of subtle flavouring. Serve well chilled with tiny crisp croûtons.

Mash the avocados and lemon juice together with a fork. Gradually blend in the stock, cumin, garlic and milk. Whisk the cream into the mixture and season generously with salt and pepper. Pour the soup into a serving bowl, cover, and chill for several hours. Adjust the seasoning before serving lightly sprinkled with the chopped chives.

Serves 4–6

CHILLED PRAWN AND AVOCADO SOUP

1 small onion
250 g peeled, cooked prawns
2½ cups sweetened tomato juice
2 cups natural yoghurt
salt
Cayenne pepper
1 small avocado
3 tablespoons tiny crisp croûtons

Put the onion and prawns through a blender, food processor or fine blade of mincer until crumbly. Transfer the mixture to a bowl, add the tomato juice and yoghurt and whisk together until no streaks remain in the liquid. Season generously with salt and Cayenne and chill for 2–3 hours. Peel and stone the avocado and cut into small dice. Adjust the seasoning of the chilled soup, if necessary, before pouring into a chilled tureen or individual bowls. Sprinkle with the avocado and croûtons before serving.

Serves 4–6

AVOCADO MEXICALI

6 cups chicken stock, or use cubes
2 medium-sized onions, sliced
½ teaspoon dried oregano
1 teaspoon curry powder
1 small chicken fillet
salt
white pepper
1 avocado, peeled, stoned and sliced
2 teaspoons finely chopped coriander or parsley

Sometimes the simplest soups are the most delicious. This is one of them.

Put the stock, onions, oregano, curry powder and the chicken into a pan. Bring very slowly to the boil, season to taste and simmer for 15 minutes, until the chicken is tender. Remove the chicken and cool slightly before cutting into thin strips. Strain the stock and discard the onion. Return the stock and chicken to the pan, add the avocado and simmer for 2–3 minutes before serving, lightly sprinkled with coriander or parsley.

Serves 6

AVOCADO AND ARTICHOKE SOUP

2 tablespoons butter
1 medium-sized onion, chopped
1 stalk celery, sliced
1 large potato, peeled and grated
1 clove garlic, crushed
1 tablespoon drained capers
2 fresh globe artichokes
4 cups chicken stock, or use cubes
2 medium-sized avocados, peeled and stoned
2 teaspoons lemon juice
salt
white pepper
¾ cup cream
small croûtons for serving

The success of this almond green soup depends on using only fresh globe artichokes.

Melt the butter in a pan, cook the onion and celery for a few minutes until softened but not browned. Add the potato, garlic and capers, stir with the onion mixture and simmer gently for 2 minutes. Trim and discard the stem and very coarse outer leaves from the artichokes. Slice the artichokes thinly and add to the pan with the stock. Bring to the boil then simmer very gently for 30 minutes. Dice the avocados, add to the soup and simmer 5 minutes. Blend or sieve the soup until smooth and put through a coarse strainer to remove any celery fibres or tough artichoke threads. Add the lemon juice, salt and pepper to taste, add the cream. Serve hot, gently reheated without boiling, or very well chilled. Garnish with crisp croûtons.

Serves 6

MEXICAN VEGETABLE SOUP

- 2 tablespoons butter
- 2 medium-sized onions, quartered and sliced
- 2 carrots, coarsely chopped
- 250 g pumpkin, peeled and chopped
- 3 large tomatoes, peeled and chopped
- 5 cups chicken stock, or use cubes
- salt
- black pepper
- 1 cup frozen or canned corn kernels
- 1 avocado, peeled, stoned and diced
- 2 tablespoons chopped coriander or parsley

Melt the butter in a large saucepan. Toss the onions, carrots and pumpkin together, cook for 10 minutes over low heat until the juices run. They need stirring occasionally. Add the tomatoes and stock, bring to the boil then simmer. Season to taste and cook until the vegetables are tender, about 40 minutes. Add the corn, avocado and coriander, adjust the seasoning and simmer for a few minutes.

Serves 6–8

TOMATO AND AVOCADO SOUP

- 1 tablespoon butter
- 1 medium-sized onion, chopped
- 1 tablespoon flour
- 1½ cups chicken stock, or use cubes
- 440 g can peeled tomatoes
- 1 bay leaf
- good pinch nutmeg
- 2 cloves
- ½ teaspoon paprika
- ½ teaspoon sugar
- salt
- black pepper
- lemon juice
- 2 medium-sized firm ripe tomatoes, peeled, seeded and chopped
- 1 avocado
- 2 tablespoons port

Melt the butter in a large pan and fry the onion until lightly browned. Stir in the flour and cook over low heat for 1 minute. Gradually add the stock, stirring until thickened. Crush the canned tomatoes with their juice, add to the pan with the bay leaf, spices and sugar. Simmer for 15 minutes. Season the soup with salt, pepper and lemon juice and simmer for a further 10 minutes. Either blend the soup until smooth in a food processor or blender, or put the soup through a sieve. Return the soup to the pan, add the chopped tomatoes and heat through. Peel, stone and slice the avocado, add to the soup with the port and heat gently for 3–4 minutes before serving.

Serves 6

COCKLE BOAT

8 cockles, approx. 1 kg, well scrubbed
3 tablespoons butter
1 medium-sized onion, chopped
2 stalks celery, sliced
1 clove garlic, finely chopped
5 cups cold water
1 bay leaf
3 sprigs parsley
1 large potato, peeled and grated
60 g smoked spek, finely diced
4 shallots, thinly sliced
2 tablespoons flour
¼ cup cream
salt
white pepper
1 avocado
paprika

Cockles are increasingly available, particularly in fish markets. Unlike the tiny cockles of the cold Northern seas, ours are large, very meaty and make excellent soup.

Cover the cockles with cold water and soak for 45 minutes. This will allow them to throw off some sand. Melt 2 tablespoons of the butter in a large saucepan, add the onion, celery and garlic. Fry gently, without browning, until the vegetables are softened. Add the water, bay leaf and parsley, bring to the boil then simmer for 10 minutes. Add the cockles and simmer until the shells open. As each cockle opens remove it from the stock and cool. Strain the stock through muslin, discard the flavouring ingredients. Return the liquid to the pan, add the potato, simmer for 10 minutes. Remove the cockles from the shells, rinse the meat under cold water to remove any sand particles. Mince or finely chop the meat and set aside. Sauté the spek in the remaining butter until the fat runs, add the shallots and cook until soft. Sprinkle the flour over the shallot mixture, stir to combine thoroughly and cook, without browning, 2 minutes. Gradually add the stock with the potato, stirring constantly until smooth. Add the cockles and simmer for 10 minutes. The soup can be prepared ahead to this stage and finished just before serving. Stir the cream into the simmering soup and season to taste. Peel, stone and slice the avocado, add to the soup and heat through. Serve very hot with a light sprinkling of paprika.

Serves 6–8

Avocados with Roquefort Sauce, page 34
Avocado slices on a piquant Roquefort and watercress dressing.

Overleaf
Guacamole
Two versions of this favourite dip, the textured Traditional Guacamole, page 13 and the creamy Californian, page 14.

Chilled Avocado Soup, page 23
A light, tangy soup for easy summer entertaining.

AVOCADO GAZPACHO

1 green capsicum, seeded and sliced
1 cucumber, peeled and seeded
500 g ripe tomatoes, peeled and seeded
2 cloves garlic, peeled
1 avocado
2 teaspoons lemon juice
1 tablespoon chopped parsley
1 tablespoon chopped mint
1½ tablespoons wine vinegar
1 tablespoon olive oil
1½ cups iced water
salt
black pepper
1 small red capsicum, seeded and finely diced
4 shallots, finely sliced
6 black olives, stoned and chopped

Put the green capsicum, cucumber, tomatoes and garlic in a blender or food processor, blend for about 1 minute until smooth. Peel and stone the avocado, brush one half with lemon juice and set aside. Chop the second avocado half roughly, add to the blender with the herbs, vinegar and oil, blend for a few seconds until smooth. Pour the mixture into a bowl, add the iced water and season to taste with salt and pepper. Cover and chill 1½–2 hours. Just before serving dice the reserved avocado and stir into the gazpacho with the remaining ingredients and a few ice cubes.

Serves 6

CRAB AND AVOCADO SOUP

2 tablespoons vegetable oil
1 tablespoon butter
1 large onion, coarsely chopped
1 green capsicum, seeded and diced
1½ tablespoons flour
400 g can peeled tomatoes
1 large clove garlic, finely chopped
finely grated rind 1 lemon
1 bay leaf
½ teaspoon Tabasco sauce
salt
black pepper
225 g fresh or canned crabmeat
1¼ cups milk
1 avocado
¼ cup cream

Heat the oil and butter in a saucepan. Add the onion and capsicum and cook over medium heat until the onion is transparent. Sprinkle the flour over the onion mixture, blend and cook gently for 2 minutes. Slice the canned tomatoes and stir into the pan with the juice, garlic, lemon rind, bay leaf and Tabasco. Season to taste, cover the pan and simmer for 10 minutes. Add the crabmeat and the milk, stir until blended and simmer 5 minutes. Peel, stone and slice the avocado crossways, add to the soup with the cream and adjust the seasoning. Simmer 2–3 minutes before serving.

Serves 6

BORSCHT WITH AVOCADO

3 medium-sized beetroots
1 small celeriac, approx. 185 g or, 2 stalks celery, thinly sliced
1 medium-sized onion, chopped
2 cloves garlic, crushed
5 cups chicken stock, or use cubes
2 tablespoons lemon juice
salt
black pepper
1 small avocado

A multiple choice soup that can be served thick or thin, hot or chilled, and all from the same batch of ingredients.

Wash the beetroots, trim the roots and leaves. Place in a pan with enough cold water to cover. Bring to the boil and simmer for 8 minutes. Strain and refresh under cold running water. Peel and grate the beetroot and celeriac, and put them in a large saucepan with the onion, garlic, chicken stock and 1 tablespoon lemon juice. Season with salt and pepper, bring to the boil then simmer, with the pan covered, until the vegetables are tender. Now you make the choice of a light or thicker soup. For the thin soup, strain and discard the vegetables. For the thicker soup, strain the soup and purée the vegetables. Stir the purée into the strained liquid. The light and thick soups are both finished in the same way. Return the soup to the pan and adjust the seasoning, peel, stone and slice the avocado thinly, add to the soup and simmer gently for 2 minutes. If serving the light soup chilled, season generously as chilling lessens flavour. Chill before adding the avocado.

Serves 6

SCALLOPED CORN AND AVOCADO SOUP

2 cups corn niblets, canned or frozen
4 cups chicken stock, or use cubes
8–12 Tasmanian scallops
1 avocado
salt
pepper
2 tablespoons cream

Combine corn and stock in a saucepan, bring to a slow boil, then simmer for 6–7 minutes. Trim the scallops, remove any dark vein but leave the coral attached. Peel and stone the avocado and brush with cold water. Strain the soup and purée the corn. Return the soup to the pan set over very low heat. Stir in the corn purée and season to taste. Add the scallops and poach in the barely simmering soup for 3 minutes. Slice the avocado thinly, add to the soup with the cream and heat through for a minute or so without boiling.

Serves 4–6

PIPI CHOWDER

1 kg pipis
2 cups cold water
2 tablespoons butter
1 medium-sized onion, chopped
2 stalks celery, chopped
1 small leek, quartered lengthways and sliced
3 medium-sized ripe tomatoes, peeled, seeded and chopped
¾ cup dry white wine
small bunch celery leaves
4 parsley stems
1 large bay leaf
½ teaspoon dried rosemary
125 g green prawns, shelled, deveined and chopped
salt
white pepper
2 tablespoons tomato paste
¼ cup cream
1 avocado, peeled, stoned and sliced

Wash the pipis, discard any with open shells and soak in cold water for 30 minutes. Put the pipis into a pan with 2 cups cold water and simmer over low heat until the shells open. Remove the pipis and cool. Strain the stock through a muslin-lined sieve. Melt the butter in a large saucepan, sauté the onion, celery and leek until softened. Add the tomatoes, stir the vegetables together and simmer for 3–4 minutes. Tie the celery leaves, parsley and bay leaf into a bouquet. Make the stock up to 4½ cups with cold water, add to the pan with the wine, bouquet and rosemary. Bring to the boil then reduce the heat until the soup is very slowly simmering. Add the prawns and season to taste. Cover and simmer for 20 minutes. Discard the bouquet. The soup can be prepared ahead to this stage and finished shortly before serving. Remove the pipis from the shells and rinse under cold water to remove any lingering sand particles. Discard any connecting valve membrane. Add the pipis to the soup. Blend the tomato paste and cream, add to the pan with the avocado and simmer 3–4 minutes. Adjust the seasoning before serving.

Serves 6–8

SPRING SUPPER SOUP

500 g tiny new potatoes, scraped
10 spring onions, trimmed and halved
2 cups chicken stock, or use cubes
1 bay leaf
small bunch celery leaves
2 cups milk
¼ small cauliflower, broken in flowerets (about 1 cup)
salt
pepper
500 g fish fillet, cut in 2.5 cm cubes
1 small avocado
3 tablespoons sour cream
paprika

Cubes of fish are poached in this light, but substantial vegetable soup. Ling fish is a good choice because it holds its shape but any thick white fish may be used.

Halve the potatoes if larger than walnut-size and place in a pan with the onions, stock, bay and celery leaves. Bring to the boil, cover and simmer for 8 minutes. Add the milk and cauliflowerets, when the soup begins to simmer again season to taste, cook for 5 minutes. Add the fish, cover the pan and simmer for 10 minutes or until the potatoes are tender. Peel, stone and slice the avocado, add to the soup and adjust the seasoning. Heat through for 1-2 minutes. Pour the soup into a hot tureen, drizzle the sour cream over and sprinkle with paprika.

Serves 6

Entrées

First impressions, with food particularly, are very important so an entrée should be tempting to the eye as well as the palate and certainly avocados are just that.

While I can see how the ubiquitous avocado vinaigrette has happened—a halved avocado presents itself neatly packaged with two perfect containers just begging to be filled—to serve a half avocado before anything but the lightest meal is courting sapped appetites, and if you must serve them this way then do choose very small avocados. However, one large avocado, sliced or cubed has stretchable qualities and will adequately serve four people instead of two.

AVOCADOS WITH ROQUEFORT SAUCE

60 g Roquefort cheese (not the processed variety)
2 egg yolks
small bunch watercress, about 12 sprigs
½ cup olive oil
juice 1 lemon
salt
white pepper
2 avocados
3 tablespoons flaked almonds, lightly toasted

Crumble the cheese and blend with the egg yolks in a food processor (use the chopping blade) or blender until smooth. Reserve a few small sprigs of watercress, add the rest of the bunch to the cheese mixture and blend. Gradually add the oil, blending until just mixed. Push the sauce through a broad meshed sieve and season to taste with lemon juice, salt and pepper. Peel and stone the avocados. Place them, cut side down, on a board and cut lengthways into thin slices. Brush the slices with lemon juice. Pour a little sauce over each serving plate and arrange overlapping slices of avocado over the sauce. Garnish the plate with a few almonds and a sprig of watercress before serving.

Serves 6, 8 if the avocados are large

AVOCADOS WITH GINGER SAUCE

¼ cup strained lemon juice
½ cup ginger wine
125 g butter, diced
2 avocados
6 pieces preserved ginger, rinsed and chopped
watercress or parsley to garnish

The sour piquant ginger sauce can also be sweetened to taste, before coating the avocados, to make a delicious light dessert.

Boil the lemon juice and ginger wine together until reduced by two thirds. Skim any brown foam from the surface of the mixture. Remove from the heat and gradually whisk in the butter. Peel, stone and slice the avocados lengthways, arrange on serving plates. Coat the avocados with sauce and top with a little of the chopped ginger. Garnish with watercress or parsley. The sauce can be prepared ahead of time and very gently reheated when needed.

Serves 4–6

STUFFED AVOCADOS

125 g farm or cream cheese
1 tablespoon natural yoghurt or sour cream
1 tablespoon very finely chopped shallots
6 green olives, stoned and very finely chopped
2 teaspoons chopped fresh basil or coriander
black pepper
lemon juice
2 medium-sized avocados
watercress or lettuce leaves for serving
¼ cup vinaigrette dressing (page 94)

Blend the cheese with the yoghurt or sour cream until smooth. Add the shallots, olives and herbs and mix well. Season with pepper and lemon juice to taste. Peel and stone the avocados, divide the filling between the cavities and press the halves firmly together. Brush the outside of the avocados with lemon juice, wrap closely with plastic film and chill for an hour or so. To serve cut the avocados, crossways, into slices about 1 cm thick, arrange on watercress or lettuce leaves and drizzle a little vinaigrette sauce over.

Serves 4–6

AVOCADOS À LA GREQUE

1/4 cup olive oil
1 medium-sized onion, finely chopped
1/4 cup tomato paste
1/3 cup dry white wine
1 clove garlic, finely chopped
pinch ground ginger
6 whole coriander seeds
2–3 teaspoons lemon juice
salt
black pepper
2 avocados
2 tablespoons chopped coriander or parsley

Heat the oil in a pan and cook the onion over low heat until transparent. Add the tomato paste, wine, garlic and spices. Mix well, bring to the boil then simmer for 10 minutes. Season generously with salt and pepper. Peel, stone and quarter the avocados, cut into 1 cm slices. Add the avocados to the sauce with lemon juice to taste. Simmer for 2 minutes and serve hot or chilled lightly sprinkled with the herbs.

Serves 4–6

AVOCADO STUFFED ZUCCHINI

6 zucchini, each 10–12 cm long
salt
1/4 teaspoon black pepper
1/4 teaspoon dry mustard
2 tablespoons lemon juice
1/3 cup olive or vegetable oil
1 medium-sized onion, finely chopped
2 cloves garlic, finely chopped
1 small green capsicum, seeded and chopped
4 shallots, thinly sliced
1 avocado, peeled, stoned and diced
1 dill pickle, chopped
2 medium-sized tomatoes, peeled, seeded and chopped
1 teaspoon finely chopped fresh basil or parsley

Have ready boiling salted water. Trim the ends off the zucchini, drop into the water and simmer 4–5 minutes until they are just beginning to soften. Drain, cool slightly before halving the zucchini lengthways. Scoop out the seeds and discard. Place the zucchini, cut side up, in a shallow dish. Blend 1/2 teaspoon salt, the pepper, mustard and lemon juice. Add the oil and whisk or shake until thick. Add the onion and garlic, stir together and pour over the zucchini. Marinate 3 hours or longer. Drain the zucchini and discard the marinade. When ready to serve combine the remaining ingredients, season to taste and spoon into the shells.

Serves 4–6

CUCUMBER AND AVOCADO APPETISER

2 cucumbers, peeled, seeded and sliced
2 tablespoons walnut or olive oil
2 tablespoons wine vinegar
½ teaspoon black pepper
1 avocado
3–4 teaspoons lemon juice
salt
¼ cup cream, lightly whipped
1 teaspoon prepared horseradish
lettuce leaves for serving
chopped watercress or parsley

Place the sliced cucumber in a bowl, add the oil, vinegar and pepper. Turn the cucumber slices in the mixture until evenly coated and marinate for a minimum of 30 minutes. Drain excess liquid from the cucumbers and chill. Peel, stone and halve the avocado, blend until smooth and add lemon juice and salt to taste. Blend the cream and horseradish, swirl lightly through the avocado purée. Arrange the cucumber on lettuce leaves, drizzle the sauce over and sprinkle with chopped watercress or parsley.

Serves 4–6

AVOCADO AND GRAPEFRUIT WITH POPPYSEED DRESSING

2 grapefruit, halved and segmented
1 large avocado, peeled, and stoned
1½ tablespoons lemon juice
2 teaspoons honey
⅛ teaspoon dry mustard
½ teaspoon salt
1½ tablespoons olive or vegetable oil
1 teaspoon poppy seeds
crisp lettuce leaves for serving

An anytime salad. Serve on crisp lettuce leaves as a first course or in the grapefruit shells for a sparkling breakfast.

Remove any bitter membrane from the grapefruit and cube the avocado. Toss lightly together in a bowl. Blend the lemon juice, honey, mustard and salt. Add the oil and poppyseeds and shake the dressing together until slightly thickened. Pour the dressing over the fruit and chill before serving.

Serves 4

HERRING AND AVOCADO TEMPTATION

3 Bismarck herrings
1 Granny Smith apple, cored and diced
1 small onion, chopped
1 stalk celery, sliced
1 avocado
salt
black pepper
crisp lettuce
½ cup light sour cream
¼ cup mayonnaise (see page 95)
paprika

Dry the herrings and slice, crossways, into 2 cm strips. Combine the herrings with the apple, onion and celery. Peel, stone and quarter the avocado, slice and brush lightly with cold water. Fork the avocado through the herring mixture and season with salt and pepper to taste. Chill thoroughly. Arrange lettuce cups on plates and fill with the herring salad. Blend the sour cream and mayonnaise, drizzle a little over each salad and serve generously sprinkled with paprika.

Serves 4–6

PEPERONI ALBERTINE

4 red capsicums
1 large avocado
2 teaspoons lemon juice
½ cup olive or vegetable oil
2½ tablespoons wine vinegar
1 teaspoon Worcestershire sauce
2 cloves garlic, very finely chopped
1 teaspoon anchovy paste
½ teaspoon paprika
½ teaspoon castor sugar
salt
black pepper

Serve as a first course or as an accompaniment with cold white meats or fish.

Preheat oven to 220°C. Put the dry capsicums on a baking tray and bake for 15–20 minutes until the skins blister. Cool slightly and peel. Quarter the capsicums, discarding the stem and seeds. Set aside. Peel, stone and slice the avocado, brush the slices lightly with lemon juice. Arrange alternate slices of avocado and capsicum quarters in a shallow serving dish. Blend the liquid ingredients with the garlic, anchovy paste, paprika and sugar, season to taste and pour over the salad. Marinate at room temperature for 1 hour. Chill before serving.

Serves 4–6

Taco Crust Pie, page 49
An unusual pie crust with a traditional taco filling.

AVOCADO TARAMA

1 small onion, very finely chopped
100 g tarama (see note below)
3 small cold boiled potatoes, peeled
2 crustless slices white bread
½ cup strained lemon juice
1 cup olive oil
2 large avocados

The robust flavour of the tarama is a marvellous complement to the avocado. You can use a commercially prepared taramosalata but with the aid of a blender it is easily prepared and the flavour infinitely better.

Blend the onion, tarama and potatoes until smooth. Soak the bread in cold water, squeeze dry and add to the potato mixture. Blend until smooth. Add the lemon juice and oil alternately, tasting as you do until all the oil is used up but not necessarily all the lemon juice. Peel, stone and slice the avocados lengthways. Brush the slices with cold water and fan onto serving plates. Spoon taramosalata across the avocado before serving. Any remaining tarama will keep for several days in the refrigerator. Cover the surface closely with plastic film.

Note Bulk packed tarama, available in most continental delicatessens, has a far superior flavour and colour to the tiny cans.

Serves 4–6

AVOCADO AND GRAPEFRUIT COCKTAIL

2 or 3 grapefruit, chilled
1 large avocado
1 tablespoon lemon juice
2 teaspoons castor sugar
3 teaspoons coarsely chopped fresh mint
2 tablespoons olive oil
salt
black pepper
2 tablespoons chopped pistachio nuts

Halve the grapefruit and remove the segments, discarding any bitter membrane. A grapefruit knife does make this job very easy. Reserve the grapefruit shells. Put the segments and juice into a bowl. Peel and stone the avocado, ball or cube the fruit and add to the grapefruit. Blend the lemon juice, sugar, mint and oil, season to taste with salt and pepper. Pour the dressing over the mixture and turn carefully to coat before piling into the grapefruit shells. Sprinkle with nuts before serving.

Serves 4–6

Creole Chicken Livers, page 46
Spicy chicken livers are complemented by the smooth avocado sauce.

MUSHROOM AND AVOCADO TARTS

2 cups flour
pinch salt
185 g butter
iced water
500 g tiny white button mushrooms
3 tablespoons butter
3 tablespoons marsala
⅓ cup cream
1 avocado
salt
white pepper

Sift the flour and salt together, rub in the butter and mix to a fairly soft dough with about 2 tablespoons of water. Cover closely with plastic film and refrigerate 1 hour. Roll the pastry thinly and line 8 × 10 cm flan tins. Prick the bases and line the pastry closely with foil. Chill for 15 minutes. Preheat the oven to 190°C. Bake the tarts for 15 minutes, remove the foil and bake for another 5 minutes until crisp. Cool on racks. If preparing the tart shells ahead of time cool completely before storing in airtight container. Wipe the mushrooms and trim the brown ends from the stalks. Heat the butter and sauté the mushrooms until just softened. Lift from the pan with a slotted spoon and keep warm. Add the marsala and cream to the pan juices and simmer gently until slightly thickened. Peel, stone and quarter the avocado. Cut crossways into 1 cm slices. Add the avocado to the sauce with the mushrooms and season to taste. Simmer for 3–4 minutes. To serve reheat the tarts briefly in a hot oven. Place a hot tart case on each plate, spoon the filling in and serve immediately.

Serves 8 as a first course, 4 as a main course or luncheon

AVOCADO MOULD

1 tablespoon gelatine
¾ cup cold water
3 small avocados
1 teaspoon drained green peppercorns, crushed
1 small onion, very finely chopped
½ teaspoon Tabasco sauce
salt
¼ cup mayonnaise (page 95)
½ cup cream, whipped
lettuce

Prepare the mould at least 6 hours before serving or overnight, and in very hot weather use an extra teaspoon of gelatine. Sprinkle the gelatine over the cold water and soak for a few minutes. Dissolve over gentle heat and strain into a mixing bowl. Cool until the gelatine is syrupy, about the consistency of fresh egg whites. Peel, stone and purée 2 of the avocados. Blend with the peppercorns, onion and Tabasco and season to taste with salt. Fold the avocado mixture, mayonnaise and cream into the gelatine and blend thoroughly. Pour the mixture into a wet ring mould and chill until set. To serve, slice the remaining avocado and garnish the centre of the mould with lettuce and avocado slices.

Serves 4–6

Main Courses

While writing this book life became rather avocado or nothing. Visitors to the house were surprised at the number of avocados in evidence and when inviting friends to dinner I did feel obliged to warn them, 'Remember it is avocado with everything.' The reply, a polite, 'That's no hardship.' And so it turned out. Avocado with everything is no hardship at all. They really are a remarkable fruit adapting to almost every circumstance and playing the multiple role in savoury cooking of adding flavour, texture and colour to the food.

PORK MEDALLIONS WITH AVOCADO

3 tablespoons butter
1 head Florence fennel, trimmed and cut into 4 slices
salt
black pepper
1 tablespoon lemon juice
500 g pork fillet, trimmed and cut into 2.5 cm slices
4 shallots, sliced
2 teaspoons tomato paste
2 teaspoons flour
¾ cup chicken stock, or use cubes
1 avocado, peeled, stoned and sliced
2 tablespoons brandy

Melt 2 tablespoons of the butter in a shallow pan. When just sizzling sauté the fennel slices for 2 to 3 minutes on each side without browning the butter. Season with salt, pepper and lemon juice. Transfer the fennel to a serving dish and keep hot. Add the shallots to the pan and cook until just softened, push them to one side of the pan and add the remaining butter. Sauté the pork slices for 4 to 5 minutes on each side, season lightly and arrange on the fennel with the shallots. Stir the flour into the pan, cook over low heat for 1 minute. Add the tomato paste, stir well and gradually add the stock. Simmer, stirring constantly until the sauce is lightly thickened and smooth. Adjust the seasoning and add the avocado and brandy. Simmer for 1 minute before spooning over the pork.

Serves 4

POLYNESIAN PORK

2 tablespoons vegetable oil
750 g lean pork, cut into 2.5 cm cubes
1 medium-sized onion, halved and sliced
1 red capsicum, seeded and sliced
2 carrots, cut in julienne strips
¾ cup seedless raisins
1½ cups veal or chicken stock, or use cubes
¼ cup lemon juice
1 tablespoon light soy sauce
2 tablespoons brown sugar
1 large clove garlic, crushed
black pepper
salt
2 tablespoons cornflour
1 large avocado
4 pineapple rings, halved

Heat the oil in a heavy pan and brown the pork cubes evenly on all sides. Toss the vegetables and raisins together, add to the pork and mix well. Blend the stock, lemon juice, soy sauce, sugar and garlic and pour over the pork. Season generously with pepper, very lightly, if at all, with salt. Cover the pan and simmer for 1 hour or until the pork is tender. Slake the cornflour with a little cold water, add to the casserole and blend thoroughly. Simmer 3 to 4 minutes before adjusting the seasoning. Peel and stone the avocado and cut crossways into fairly thick slices. Add the avocado and pineapple to the pan and simmer gently until heated through.

Serves 4–6

STIR FRIED PORK WITH AVOCADO

3 tablespoons vegetable oil
2 cloves garlic, peeled
60 g walnut halves
1 leek, halved lengthways and sliced
2 stalks celery, sliced
400 g pork fillet, cut in 1 cm slices
¾ cup bean sprouts
salt
1 teaspoon chilli sauce
1 avocado, peeled, stoned and sliced

Serve with buttered pasta or rice.

Heat the oil in a large, shallow pan or wok and sauté the garlic cloves for 2 minutes. Remove and discard the garlic. Add the walnuts to the pan and cook over medium heat until lightly browned. Remove the nuts and set aside. Stir fry the leeks and celery in the hot fat for 2 to 3 minutes. Add the pork and cook, turning constantly, for 3 to 4 minutes. Add the bean sprouts, salt and chilli sauce, turn the ingredients together until thoroughly mixed. Fork the sliced avocado through and cook over low heat for 2 minutes. Serve immediately.

Serves 4–6

PAN BRAISED VEAL CUTLETS WITH AVOCADO

1 tablespoon vegetable oil
1 tablespoon butter
750 g veal cutlets
1 medium-sized onion, diced
1 stalk celery, thinly sliced
1½ tablespoons flour
2 tablespoons tomato paste
1½ cups veal or chicken stock, or use cubes
salt
black pepper
2 cloves garlic, finely chopped
1 avocado
1 tablespoon finely chopped parsley

Heat the oil and butter together and quickly brown the cutlets on both sides. Remove from the pan. Add the onion and celery and cook over medium heat until pale golden. Sprinkle the flour over the vegetables, stir until blended and cook for 1 minute. Add the tomato paste and stock, stirring until the sauce is smooth. Season to taste with salt and pepper. Stir the garlic into the sauce and return the cutlets to the pan, spooning some of the sauce over each one. Cover and simmer 30 minutes or until the meat is tender. Peel, stone and slice the avocado and add to the pan. Simmer for a further 3 minutes before serving sprinkled with the parsley.

Serves 4–6

VEAL STEAKS WITH SAUCE VERTE

1 small avocado, peeled and stoned
2 tablespoons capers, drained and mashed
1 teaspoon green peppercorns
1 tablespoon lemon juice
salt
black pepper
4 leg veal steaks
1 tablespoon flour
1 egg
1 tablespoon water
¾ cup dry breadcrumbs
3 tablespoons butter
1 tablespoon vegetable oil

Mash or purée the avocado, add the capers and peppercorns and season to taste with lemon juice, salt and pepper. Set aside. Trim any membrane from the edge of the veal steaks and pound with a meat hammer or rolling pin until thin. Combine flour with ½ teaspoon salt and pepper. Dust veal lightly with the flour, shaking off any excess. Beat the egg and water together, dip the veal into the egg mixture and then into the crumbs. Chill for a few minutes to allow the coating to firm. Melt the butter with the oil in a shallow pan. Sauté the veal for 2–3 minutes on each side. Serve very hot accompanied by the avocado sauce.

Serves 4

KIDNEY DEVIL WITH AVOCADO

- 10 lamb kidneys, skinned, cored and quartered
- 1 tablespoon butter
- 1 tablespoon vegetable oil
- 1½ tablespoons flour
- ½ cup chicken stock
- ¾ cup milk
- 2 tablespoons French mustard
- salt
- black pepper
- 1 avocado, peeled, stoned and diced
- 2 tablespoons chopped parsley

Even those who do not usually enjoy kidneys seem to find them appealing with the avocado and devil sauce.

Melt the butter with the oil, add the kidneys and turn in the hot fat until evenly coated. Stirring occasionally, cook the kidneys for 4 to 5 minutes. Remove from the pan with a slotted spoon and keep warm. Stir the flour into the pan juices and cook over low heat for 1 minute. Gradually add the stock and milk, stirring between each addition until the sauce is smooth and thickened. Stir in the mustard and season to taste. Simmer 2 to 3 minutes. Return the kidneys to the sauce with the avocado and parsley. Simmer for 2 minutes longer and adjust the seasoning before serving.

Serves 4–6

CREOLE CHICKEN LIVERS

- 1 large avocado
- 2–3 teaspoons lemon juice
- ½ teaspoon Worcestershire sauce
- ½ teaspoon Tabasco sauce
- 3 tablespoons cream
- salt
- 1 tablespoon butter
- 2 tablespoons olive or vegetable oil
- 500 g chicken livers, skinned and trimmed
- 2–3 fresh hot chilli peppers, seeded and very thinly sliced
- 2 cloves garlic, finely chopped
- 2 tablespoons cold water
- black pepper
- 2 tablespoons chopped coriander or parsley

Prepare the sauce first. Peel and stone the avocado, blend with the lemon juice, sauces and cream. Season to taste and set aside. Melt the butter with the oil in a shallow pan. Turn the livers in the hot fat until sealed. Add the chillies, garlic and water, stir together and season to taste with salt and a little pepper. Cover the pan and simmer, giving the livers a stir occasionally, for 6–7 minutes. Transfer the livers to a heated serving dish and sprinkle with coriander. Spoon some of the sauce over the livers and serve the rest separately.

Serves 4–6

CHICKEN AND AVOCADO GOUGÈRE

1 quantity Choux Pastry (page 85)
1 tablespoon butter
1 tablespoon vegetable oil
1 medium-sized onion chopped
100 g smoked spek or ham, diced
250 g boneless chicken, cut in 1 cm strips
125 g mushrooms, sliced
¼ teaspoon celery seeds
salt
black pepper
1 tablespoon flour
1 cup chicken stock, or use cubes
2 tablespoons dry sherry
1 avocado

Prepare the choux pastry and allow to become cold at room temperature. Preheat the oven to 200°C and lightly oil a 23 cm circular baking dish or ring mould. Spoon the pastry around the edge of the baking dish leaving the centre free. Bake for 35 minutes or until the pastry is crisp and golden. While the pastry is cooking melt the butter with the oil in a shallow pan. Sauté the onion until pale golden in colour, add the spek or ham and cook over medium heat until the fat runs. Add the chicken, stir with the onion mixture and cook for 5–6 minutes. Stir in the mushrooms and celery seeds, season lightly with salt and pepper and cook gently for 4–5 minutes. Sprinkle the flour over the chicken mixture, stir until well blended and cook for 1 minute. Gradually add the stock, stirring constantly until the sauce is smooth and lightly thickened. Add the sherry and simmer, uncovered, for a few minutes. Peel, stone and slice the avocado, add to the pan and adjust the seasoning. Simmer over very low heat for 2 minutes. To serve, arrange the hot pastry ring on a serving dish and spoon the filling into the centre.

Serves 4–6

CHICKEN CAPRICORNIA

1.5 kg chicken pieces
½ teaspoon salt
¼ teaspoon black pepper
1 tablespoon flour
2 tablespoons butter
1 tablespoon vegetable oil
225 g can lychees
1½ cups fresh orange juice
1 teaspoon light soy sauce
¼ teaspoon ground cinnamon
2 whole cloves
1 tablespoon cornflour
1 avocado
finely grated rind ½ orange

Skin the chicken if you prefer. Mix the salt, pepper and flour together, use to lightly dust the chicken. Melt the butter with the oil in a pan and brown the chicken pieces on all sides. Blend ⅓ cup of the lychee syrup with the orange juice, soy and cinnamon. Add to the pan with the strained lychees and cloves. Cover and simmer 45–50 minutes or until the chicken is tender. With a slotted spoon transfer the chicken and lychees to a heated serving dish. Slake the cornflour with a little cold water, stir into the sauce and bring to a slow boil. Adjust the seasoning and simmer 3–4 minutes. Peel, stone and slice the avocado, add to the sauce and very gently heat through. Spoon the avocado slices and sauce over the chicken and serve lightly sprinkled with orange rind.

Serves 4–6

CHICKEN AND AVOCADO CASSEROLE

- 1.5 kg chicken, cut into serving pieces
- 2 tablespoons flour
- 2 teaspoons salt
- ¼ teaspoon white pepper
- ¼ teaspoon powdered rosemary
- finely grated rind 1 lemon
- 2 tablespoons vegetable oil
- 2 tablespoons butter
- 1 large onion, chopped
- 2 stalks celery, thinly sliced
- 2 teaspoons cornflour
- 1 cup chicken stock
- ½ cup vermouth or dry white wine
- 1 avocado
- 2 tablespoons cream

Preheat the oven to 190°C. Skin the chicken pieces. Combine the flour, salt, pepper, rosemary and lemon rind. Dust the chicken liberally with the seasoned flour. Heat the oil and butter in a shallow frying pan and brown the chicken on all sides. Transfer to a lidded casserole. Toss the onion and celery together, brown lightly in the frying pan. Sprinkle the cornflour over the vegetables, stir to combine and cook for 1 minute. Gradually add the stock and wine, stirring constantly until the sauce is smooth and lightly thickened. Simmer gently for 2 minutes and season to taste with salt and pepper. Pour the sauce over the chicken, cover and cook for 1 hour, or until the chicken is tender. Peel and stone the avocado, cut lengthways into thin slices. Arrange the avocado over the chicken, drizzle with the cream and cook, with the casserole covered, for 5 minutes longer.

Serves 4–5

BEEF AND AVOCADO NIÇOISE

- 2 tablespoons olive oil
- 3 medium-sized onions, thinly sliced
- 3 rashers bacon, cut into 1 cm strips
- 1 kg lean chuck steak, cubed
- 3½ tablespoons flour
- ½ cup beef stock, or use cubes
- 1 cup dry white wine
- 440 g can peeled tomatoes
- ¼ teaspoon dried marjoram
- 1 bay leaf
- 2.5 cm strip orange peel
- 2 large cloves garlic, crushed
- salt
- black pepper
- 2 large tomatoes, peeled and quartered
- 1 avocado
- 100 g black olives

Heat the oil in a large pan. Sauté the onions until lightly browned, add the bacon strips and cook until the fat runs. Lift the onions and bacon from the pan and set aside. Brown the meat on all sides, sprinkle the flour over and cook 1 minute. Gradually add the stock and wine, stirring to form a smooth sauce. Add the whole can of tomatoes, including the juice, the herbs, finely pared orange rind and the garlic. Season lightly with salt, more generously with pepper. Cover the pan and simmer 1 hour. Stir the reserved onion mixture into the beef with the quartered tomatoes. Cover the pan and simmer for a further 30 minutes or until the meat is tender. Peel and stone the avocado, cut crossways into half circles. Add the avocado slices and olives to the casserole and simmer, uncovered, for 5 minutes.

Serves 4–6

TACO CRUST PIE

½ cup flour, less 1 tablespoon
½ teaspoon baking powder
pinch salt
60 g firm butter, cut in small dice
1 egg, lightly beaten
½ cup sour cream
2 tablespoons vegetable oil
1 medium-sized onion, chopped
500 g minced lean beef
¾–1 teaspoon ground chilli
salt
325 g can red kidney beans, rinsed and drained
½ cup tomato paste
½ cup grated Cheddar cheese
1 medium-sized avocado, sliced
½ cup shredded lettuce

An easily made and interesting pie crust. The spicy filling is well complemented by the traditional taco topping.

Grease and flour a shallow 23 cm cake tin. Sift flour, baking powder and salt into a bowl. Add the diced butter. Blend the egg and sour cream together, add to the bowl. Combine all the ingredients, this will form a very soft and sticky dough. Dump all of the dough in the centre of the tin and with a spatula spread the dough thinly over the base and thickly up the sides of the tin. The crust can be prepared well in advance of the filling and refrigerated. Cook the onion in hot oil until lightly browned. Add the beef, mix well with the onion, and brown. Drain excess fat from the pan and season to taste with chilli and salt. Add the beans and tomato paste, stir to combine and simmer over very low heat for 35–40 minutes. Stir the meat occasionally because the mixture is quite thick. Adjust the seasoning before spooning the filling into the crust. Preheat the oven to 210°C and bake the pie for 20 minutes or until the crust is crisp and golden brown. Arrange the cheese, avocado and lettuce over the pie before serving.

Serves 4–6

LAMB AND AVOCADO IN CREAM SAUCE

3 tablespoons butter
1 kg lean leg or shoulder lamb cut in 1 cm strips
3 teaspoons cornflour
¾ cup chicken stock, or use cubes
¾ cup dry white wine
salt
white pepper
¼ cup cream
1 avocado, peeled, stoned and sliced
2 teaspoons chopped fresh mint

Melt 2 tablespoons of the butter in a shallow pan and sauté the lamb strips, a few at a time, until browned on the outside but still slightly pink in the centre, about 6 minutes. Transfer each batch of lamb to a dish and keep hot until all the meat has been browned. Add the remaining butter to the pan, sprinkle with the cornflour and stir together. Cook for 1 minute over low heat. Gradually add the stock and wine, stirring constantly to form a smooth, light sauce. Season to taste and simmer for 2 to 3 minutes. Add the cream. Return the lamb to the pan, stir and simmer gently for 3 to 4 minutes. Add the avocado and mint and heat gently without boiling for another minute. Adjust the seasoning before serving.

Serves 4–6

Here are five recipes using avocados as stuffing. Not a new idea, Mexicans have been doing it for centuries. The fruit adds an unusual flavour and retains its colour, and because it is insulated against direct heat does not become bitter.

TURKEY WITH AVOCADO STUFFING

5 kg turkey, with giblets
1½ cups fresh breadcrumbs
3 teaspoons dried marjoram
3 tablespoons butter
100 g bacon, chopped
1 large onion, coarsely chopped
1 avocado
1 cup seedless raisins
salt
black pepper
2 eggs, lightly beaten
1 tablespoon flour
2 tablespoons port or brandy

The stuffing is also good with duck and chicken. This quantity is sufficient for two medium-sized ducks or chickens.

Put the giblets and neck (not the liver) into a saucepan with 2½ cups of cold water, bring to the boil then simmer, with the pan covered, for 30 minutes. Strain and reserve the stock. Combine the crumbs and marjoram, set aside. Melt the butter and cook the bacon until the fat runs, add the onion and cook until transparent. Sprinkle the crumb mixture over the onions mixing thoroughly to absorb all the pan juices. Turn into a mixing bowl and cool. Peel and stone the avocado, cut into 2 cm dice and add to the crumb mixture, with the raisins. Season generously with salt and pepper. Add only enough of the egg to form a fairly crumbly stuffing. Preheat the oven to 180°C. Spoon the stuffing into the bird cavities and seal with coarse thread or small skewers. Fold the legs under the breast and tie the legs together. Brush the bird lightly with a little oil or butter and cover the breast and legs with foil. Roast for 2½–3 hours, basting occasionally. Remove the foil for the last 20 minutes of the cooking period. (If you prick the thickest part of a thigh with a skewer, the juices will run clear, not pink, when the turkey is cooked.) Transfer the turkey to a heated carving dish and cover loosely with foil. Skim the fat from the pan juices, stir the flour into the residue and cook over low heat until lightly browned. Gradually add 1 cup of the reserved stock, stirring constantly to form a smooth sauce. Add more stock to bring the sauce to a consistency you like. Season to taste and add the port or brandy. Simmer 3–4 minutes, strain and serve with the turkey.

Serves 6–8

PORK AND AVOCADO PUFF PIE

375 g puff pastry
1 medium-sized onion, chopped
1 tablespoon butter
salt
black pepper
400 g lean pork, finely minced
¼ teaspoon celery seed
1 teaspoon dried sage
2 tablespoons sultanas
1 egg, lightly beaten
1 avocado

Roll the pastry to a 23 × 13 cm rectangle and set aside. Preheat the oven to 220°C. Cook the onion in butter until transparent, season generously with salt and pepper. Combine the onion with the pork, celery seed, sage and sultanas and bind with 2 tablespoons of the egg. Place half of the pork mixture along the centre of the pastry. Peel and stone the avocado, cut in thick wedges and place on the pork. Cover with the remaining pork and press firmly to form a roll. Fold one side of the pastry over the filling, brush the edge with the beaten egg and fold the other side over. Press the join lightly to seal. Put the roll, with the join underneath, on a baking sheet. Brush the top with egg and make 4 or 5 cuts across the top to allow the steam to escape. Bake for 45 minutes until well puffed and golden. Serve hot or cold.

Serves 6

STUFFED CHICKEN BREASTS

1 small avocado, peeled and stoned
¼ cup lemon juice
½ cup fresh white breadcrumbs
½ teaspoon salt
¼ teaspoon white pepper
4 chicken fillets
½ cup grated Gruyère or Emmentaler cheese
1 egg, lightly beaten
3 tablespoons butter

Cut the avocado into 8 slices and brush lightly with some of the lemon juice. Combine the crumbs, salt and pepper and set aside. Split the chicken fillets through each centre, pound flat without tearing the meat. Brush the cut surface of the chicken with lemon juice. Divide the cheese between the chicken, top with 2 slices of avocado and fold the fillets in half over the filling. Secure the fillets with toothpicks. Dip the chicken in the egg and then the crumbs. Heat the butter in a shallow pan and brown the fillets on both sides. Reduce the heat and cook the chicken for 6–7 minutes on each side with the pan covered.

Serves 4

STUFFED LOIN OF VEAL

- 2 kg veal loin, weight before boning
- 2 tablespoons butter
- 2 tablespoons vegetable oil
- 1 small onion, finely chopped
- 1 clove garlic, crushed
- 3 spinach leaves (silver beet) shredded
- ¼ cup mixed dried fruit
- 1 slice crustless bread, crumbed
- 3 teaspoons chopped fresh thyme, or ¾ teaspoon dried thyme
- pinch ground mace
- finely grated rind 1 lemon
- 2 tablespoons lemon juice
- 1 avocado, peeled, stoned and diced
- salt
- black pepper
- ⅓ cup dry white wine
- 2 tablespoons tomato paste
- 1 cup veal stock, made with the bones
- 2 tablespoons cream
- 1 tablespoon marsala or port

Bone, or have the butcher bone, the loin. Cover the bones with cold water, bring to the boil, cover and simmer while the veal is cooking. Place the veal, skin side down, on a board and flatten slightly with a rolling pin. Melt half the butter and oil in a shallow pan and cook the onion until transparent. Add the garlic, spinach and dried fruit, simmer gently until the spinach has wilted. Remove the pan from the heat, stir in the crumbs, thyme, mace, lemon rind and juice. Season to taste and add the avocado. Combine thoroughly. Lightly season the cut side of the veal, spread the stuffing over and roll in Swiss roll fashion. Secure at intervals with string or fine skewers. Preheat the oven to 180°C. Heat the remaining butter and oil, brown the veal lightly on all sides and transfer to a baking dish. Add the wine and bake for 1–1¼ hours. Transfer the meat to a heated serving dish. Stir the tomato paste into the pan juices, add the stock and simmer 3–4 minutes. Stir in the cream and marsala, simmer gently for 1 minute. Season to taste before serving with the sliced veal.

Serves 6

STUFFED HAM STEAKS WITH CREAM SAUCE

- 4–6 ham steaks, about 1 cm thick
- 2 tablespoons butter
- 4 shallots, white and some green, chopped
- 60 g mushrooms, chopped
- 1 hard-boiled egg, chopped
- 1 small avocado, peeled, stoned and diced
- 1 teaspoon French mustard
- 3 teaspoons chopped fresh tarragon
- pepper
- ¼ cup dry white wine
- ½ cup cream

Using a sharp knife cut a pocket through the centre of each steak without cutting right through. Set aside. Melt half the butter in a frying pan large enough to hold all of the steaks. Add the shallots and mushrooms, cook over low heat until just softened. Transfer the mixture to a basin and set the pan aside. Combine the mushroom mixture, egg, avocado, mustard and half of the tarragon. (If using dried herbs reduce the quantity to 1 scant teaspoon.) Season the stuffing generously with pepper. Spoon some of the stuffing into each ham pocket and close with a toothpick. Add the remaining butter to the pan and sauté the steaks over medium heat for 3–4 minutes on each side. Transfer the steaks to a heated serving dish. Stir the wine, cream and remaining tarragon into the pan, bring to the boil, simmer for 2–3 minutes until lightly thickened. Adjust seasoning before serving with the ham.

Serves 4–6

TROUT WITH AVOCADO HOLLANDAISE

- 4 medium-sized trout, ready to cook
- 4 shallots, coarsely chopped
- 1 bay leaf, crumbled
- ¾ cup white wine
- cold water
- 1 quantity Blender Hollandaise Sauce (page 95)
- 1 small avocado, peeled, stoned and puréed
- 2–3 teaspoons lemon juice
- salt
- white pepper
- watercress or parsley sprigs to garnish

Preheat the oven to 150°C. Place the trout in a buttered baking dish with the shallots, bayleaf and wine. Add enough cold water to barely cover the fish. Cover the dish loosely with greaseproof paper or foil and bake for 20 minutes, or until the trout are just tender, but be very careful not to overcook. Prepare the hollandaise, add the avocado purée and blend smoothly. Keep the sauce warm over gently simmering water. Lift the trout from the baking dish and carefully remove the skin. Arrange on a heated serving dish and keep warm. Strain the liquid in which the fish were poached, boil rapidly until reduced by half. Stir 2–3 tablespoons of the reduced liquid into the sauce and sharpen with lemon juice to taste. Adjust the seasoning, spoon a little over each fish and serve the rest separately.

Serves 4

FISH CUTLETS MARTINIQUE

- 4 or 6 fish cutlets, tuna, jewfish, gemfish
- 1 cup fresh lemon juice
- 2 teaspoons chilli sauce
- pinch ground allspice
- 3 cloves garlic, finely chopped
- 1 teaspoon salt
- black pepper
- 1–2 tablespoons flour
- 2 tablespoons butter
- 2 tablespoons vegetable oil
- 2 stalks celery, thinly sliced
- 8 shallots, diagonally sliced
- ¼ teaspoon dried marjoram
- ½ cup water
- ½ cup dry white wine
- 1 tablespoon drained fine capers, not the large capers
- 1 avocado, peeled, stoned and sliced
- 1 tablespoon finely sliced shallot tops

Put the fish into a shallow dish in one layer. Combine ¾ cup lemon juice, chilli sauce, allspice, garlic, salt and a little pepper. Pour over the fish. Add enough cold water to just cover the cutlets and marinate for 1 hour. Drain and dry the fish, discard the marinade. Dust the cutlets lightly with flour. Heat the butter and oil together in a large pan and brown the cutlets lightly on each side. Remove from the pan and reserve. Sauté the celery and shallots until softened, add a little more butter and oil if necessary. Season lightly with salt and pepper and add the marjoram. Replace the fish in the pan, add the water and wine. Cover and simmer gently 10–15 minutes or until the fish flakes easily. Transfer the cutlets to a heated serving dish. Add the capers to the sauce with the remaining lemon juice, adjust the seasoning. Add the avocado slices and heat through. Spoon the sauce and avocado over the fish and sprinkle with shallots.

Serves 4–6

FISH CUTLETS WITH AVOCADO SAUCE

2 medium-sized onions
6 cloves
2 small carrots, thickly sliced
1 stalk celery, sliced
2 bay leaves
6 peppercorns
1 teaspoon salt
5 cups water
½ cup white wine
2 tablespoons wine vinegar
4–6 thick fish cutlets, e.g. gemfish, jewfish
2 medium-sized avocados, peeled, stoned and mashed
2 small tomatoes, peeled, seeded and chopped
2 teaspoons very finely chopped onion
3 teaspoons olive oil
lemon juice
1 teaspoon Tabasco sauce
black pepper

Stick the onions with the cloves and place into a large pan with the carrots, celery, bay leaves, peppercorns and salt. Add the water, wine and vinegar, bring to the boil then simmer, covered, for 30 minutes. Carefully lay the cutlets in the stock. Reduce the heat so that the stock is barely trembling. Poach the fish for 15–20 minutes, depending on the thickness of the cutlets. If the fish is to be served cold allow it to cool in the stock before chilling. To make the sauce, blend the avocados, tomatoes and onion until smooth. Add the oil, lemon juice to taste and the Tabasco. Season with salt and pepper. Transfer the fish to a serving platter, spoon a little of the sauce over each cutlet and serve the rest separately.

Serves 4–6

SCALLOPS BASQUAIS

4 tablespoons butter
6 shallots, green and white parts sliced
750 g scallops
¼ cup brandy
2 tablespoons tomato paste
1 clove garlic, crushed
1 tablespoon water
¼ cup dry white wine
salt
black pepper
1 avocado

Melt the butter in a shallow pan, cook the shallots until softened but not browned. Add the scallops, turn in the butter and cook gently for 5 minutes. Warm the brandy, flame and pour over the scallops. Blend the tomato paste, garlic, water and wine, add to the pan and season with salt and pepper. Simmer for 2 minutes. Peel, stone and slice the avocado, add to the scallops, simmer gently for a further 2 minutes.

Serves 4 as a main course, 8 as an appetiser

CIOPPINO

2½ tablespoons olive oil
3 large onions, halved and sliced
2 cloves garlic, chopped
440 g can peeled tomatoes
1 cup tomato paste
1 cup water
1 cup dry white wine
2 bay leaves
½ teaspoon dried oregano
salt
black pepper
750 g firm white fish fillets
500 g shelled green prawns
12 or more mussels
125 g Tasmanian scallops
1 large avocado, peeled, stoned and sliced
juice and finely grated rind ½ lemon
2 tablespoons finely chopped coriander or parsley

The quantities given here are quite substantial, although they certainly can be halved, but this is not an everyday dish and is well worth sharing.

Heat the oil in a large heatproof casserole and sauté the onions until golden. Add the garlic, crushed tomatoes and their juice, stir well and simmer. Blend the tomato paste, water and wine, add to the pan with the herbs. Stir to blend thoroughly and season. Cover the pan and simmer the sauce for 45 minutes. Cut the fish in serving portions and halve the prawns if large. Add to the sauce and simmer for 15 minutes. Scrub and debeard the mussels. Stir the scallops into the pan, add the avocado slices and lay the mussels on top. Cover and simmer over very low heat until the mussels open. Sharpen the sauce with lemon juice and adjust the seasoning. Combine the lemon rind and coriander and sprinkle over the cioppino before serving. Serve with plenty of crusty bread to soak up the sauce.

Serves 8

LOBSTER WITH WHISKY SAUCE

2 small cooked lobsters, halved
4 tablespoons butter
60 g pecan nuts
¼ cup lemon juice
¼ cup whisky
1 tablespoon chopped fresh dill, or 1 teaspoon dried dill tips
salt
black pepper
1 avocado

Remove the lobster meat from the shells, discard the feathery grey filters and cut the meat into bite-sized pieces. Set aside. Brown the nuts in hot butter, remove from the pan with a slotted spoon and reserve with the lobster. Stir the lemon juice, whisky and dill into the butter, season to taste and simmer gently for 2 minutes. Peel, stone and quarter the avocado. Cut crossways into slices. Add the lobster, nuts and avocado to the sauce, heat through very gently. Pile the mixture into the shells, drizzle with a little of the sauce and serve immediately.

Serves 4

LOMBARDY RISOTTO

90 g butter
2 medium-sized onions, chopped
1 large clove garlic, crushed
1 stalk celery, thinly sliced
1½ cups long-grain rice
2 cups hot chicken stock, or use cubes
good pinch saffron
salt
white pepper
⅓ cup very dry sherry or white wine
1 avocado, peeled, stoned and sliced
3 tablespoons freshly grated Parmesan cheese

Fresh green avocado buried in golden, buttery rice is excellent by itself or with the addition of a few chopped prawns or ham.

Melt the butter in a large, deep frying pan or wok. Add the onions, garlic and celery and cook over very low heat until soft but not at all coloured. Add the rice and mix thoroughly to coat each grain with butter. Fry gently for 4–5 minutes until the rice becomes opaque. Now add the hot stock, seasoning and saffron. Mix well and turn the heat to the lowest level. Half cover the pan and cook until all the liquid has been absorbed. Add the sherry or wine, fork through the rice and hold on low heat until all the moisture has disappeared, about 15 minutes. Fork the avocado and Parmesan through the rice and serve immediately.

Serves 6

BAKED AVOCADO WITH CRABMEAT

2 tablespoons butter
1 small onion, finely chopped
1 stalk celery, chopped
60 g button mushrooms, thinly sliced
200 g cooked crabmeat, fresh, frozen or canned
salt
black pepper
2 or 3 avocados, halved and stoned
2 teaspoons lemon juice
1 quantity Blender Hollandaise Sauce (page 95)
finely chopped parsley

This very rich dish is suitable for a lunch or before a very light dinner. The filling is adequate for 2 large or 3 smaller avocados.

Preheat the oven to 200°C. Melt the butter in a saucepan and gently cook the onion and celery until softened. Add the mushrooms and simmer 2–3 minutes. Flake the crabmeat, if using canned crab drain thoroughly before using. Add the crabmeat to the onion mixture, season to taste and cook over low heat for a few minutes. Brush the cut surface of the avocados with lemon juice and place, cut side up, in a shallow dish containing 1 cm hot water. Bake for 10 minutes. Prepare the hollandaise sauce. Fold the crab mixture into the sauce, and adjust the seasoning. Transfer the avocados to a serving dish, spoon the filling over the cavities and serve lightly sprinkled with parsley.

Serves 4–6

Baked Avocado with Crabmeat, page 56
Hot avocado in the shell with a rich crabmeat filling.

SEAFOOD AND AVOCADO WITH CREAM SAUCE

1/3 cup flaked almonds
60 g butter
1 small onion, thinly sliced
125 g button mushrooms, sliced
2 tablespoons flour
1/4 teaspoon dry mustard
1/2 teaspoon finely chopped fresh thyme, or pinch dried thyme
1 1/4 cups milk
1/2 cup cream
1 egg yolk
60 g Gruyère cheese, grated
1/4 cup vermouth or dry white wine
salt
white pepper
2–3 teaspoons lemon juice
200 g fresh, frozen or canned lobster cut into bite-sized pieces
2 × 225 g cans chunky tuna, drained
3–4 medium-sized avocados

This is a very rich dish which can be served in the shells as a luncheon or before a very light dinner, but I prefer it with a little rice and a very crisp salad as a main course.

Toast the almonds and set aside. Melt the butter in a shallow pan and sauté the onion until golden. Add the mushrooms and cook until softened. Remove the mushroom mixture with a slotted spoon and set aside. Stir the flour, mustard and thyme into the pan, blend with the pan juices until smooth and cook over low heat for 1 minute. Gradually add the milk and cream, stirring to form a smooth sauce. Simmer gently 2–3 minutes. Blend a little of the sauce with the egg yolk, stir the mixture into the sauce, add the cheese and stir over very low heat until melted. Add the vermouth and season to taste with salt, pepper and lemon juice. Fold the lobster, tuna and reserved mushroom mixture into the sauce with half the almonds. Cover and simmer over very low heat for 2 minutes. Peel, stone and cube the avocados, add to the pan and stir until evenly coated with the sauce, simmer for 2–3 minutes. Serve sprinkled with the remaining almonds.

Serves 6–8

Cioppino, page 55
Seafood and avocado casserole in a robust sauce.

Salads

The growing awareness of our need for vitamins, minerals and fibre, together with our busy lives, means that salads are playing an increasingly large part in our diet.

As a starter, an accompaniment, a light lunch or a refresher between courses, a salad is instantly transformed by the addition of avocado into something deliciously special which as a bonus supplies many of our nutritional needs.

POTATO AND AVOCADO SALAD

750 g new potatoes
4 spring onions, sliced
2 dill pickles, coarsely chopped
salt
white pepper
⅔ cup mayonnaise (page 95)
2 tablespoons white wine vinegar
1 large avocado
2 teaspoons lemon juice
60 g pecan nuts, coarsely chopped
1 teaspoon chopped fresh rosemary

Boil the new potatoes in their skins until just tender. Peel and slice if large. Toss the potatoes, onions and pickles together in a bowl. Season generously with salt and pepper. Blend the mayonnaise and vinegar. Peel and stone the avocado, cut into thick slices and add to the salad with the mayonnaise. Fold the salad together and chill before serving sprinkled with the nuts and rosemary.

Serves 6

AVOCADO PROVENÇALE

1 green capsicum, seeded and thinly sliced
lettuce
2 avocados
¼ cup vinaigrette dressing (page 94)
1 tablespoon drained capers, chopped
60 g black olives, stoned
finely chopped parsley

Blanch the sliced capsicum in boiling water for 2 minutes. Drain and cool. Peel, stone and slice the avocados lengthways, place in a shallow dish with the capsicum. Combine the dressing with the capers, pour over the avocado mixture and chill. Line a salad bowl with some of the lettuce leaves, break the rest into bite-sized pieces. Toss the avocado mixture with the broken lettuce and olives, arrange in the bowl and sprinkle lightly with parsley.

Serves 4–6

CURRIED RICE AND AVOCADO SALAD

1 tablespoon butter
1 tablespoon vegetable oil
1 large onion, coarsely chopped
1 stalk celery, thinly sliced
½ teaspoon each turmeric and ground coriander, or 1 teaspoon curry powder
1 avocado
2 cups cooked long-grain rice
¼ cup mixed dried fruit
½ cup drained pineapple chunks
2–3 tablespoons vinaigrette dressing (page 94)
2 teaspoons finely chopped fresh mint
30 g pinenuts, lightly toasted

Heat the butter and oil together, cook the onion until transparent, add the celery and cook until just softened. Sprinkle the turmeric and coriander, or curry powder, over the onion mixture and cook 1 minute. Remove from the heat and cool. Peel, stone and dice the avocado, brush the dice lightly with cold water. Fork the avocado, rice, dried fruit, pineapple and cooled onion mixture together. Arrange in a salad bowl and chill. Just before serving moisten the salad with vinaigrette and sprinkle with the mint and pinenuts.

Serves 6

TUNA AND AVOCADO SALAD

125 g haricot beans, soaked overnight in cold water
salt
1 avocado
1 small onion, very thinly sliced
225 g can tuna, drained and flaked
12 black olives, stoned
black pepper
¼ cup vinaigrette dressing (page 94)
1 teaspoon finely chopped fresh basil, or ¼ teaspoon dried basil
1 bunch watercress or lettuce leaves

Rinse the soaked beans, cover with fresh cold water, add 1 teaspoon salt and bring slowly to the boil. Cover the pan and simmer 50–60 minutes or until the beans are tender. Drain and cool under cold running water. Peel, stone and quarter the avocado, cut crossways into 1 cm slices. Carefully mix the avocado, onion, tuna, olives and beans, season to taste and place in a bowl. Combine the vinaigrette and basil, pour over the salad and chill. Pick the watercress over, discard excess stem and discoloured leaves. Arrange the watercress on a platter, pile the salad on top and drizzle any dressing left in the bowl over the watercress.

Serves 4–6

CRAB AND AVOCADO FUSILLI

200 g spiral pasta
salt
1 large avocado, peeled, stoned and diced
2 teaspoons lemon juice
200 g cooked crabmeat or prawns
2 teaspoons grated root ginger
black pepper
¾ cup mayonnaise (page 95)
2 tablespoons finely snipped chives

Cook the pasta in boiling salted water to the *al dente* stage, about 7 minutes. Rinse thoroughly in cold water. Turn the avocado in lemon juice, add to the pasta with the crab, or prawns, and ginger. Fork the mixture together and season to taste. Fold the mayonnaise and half of the chives through the salad. Chill before serving sprinkled with the remaining chives.

Serves 4–6

AVOCADO GODDESS SALAD

2 medium-sized avocados, peeled and stoned
½ cup light sour cream
½ cup mayonnaise (page 95)
3 teaspoons lemon juice
2 teaspoons white wine vinegar
¼ cup finely chopped parsley
1 teaspoon dried tarragon
1 small clove garlic, crushed
3 spring onions, very finely chopped, including some of the green tops
salt
black pepper
50 g red caviar
1 large lettuce
500 g cooked peeled prawns, approx. 900 g unpeeled weight

This variation of green goddess salad makes a very good first course or luncheon.

Purée the avocado and blend with the sour cream, mayonnaise, lemon juice and vinegar. Add the herbs, garlic and onions and season to taste with salt and pepper. Fold the caviar gently through the sauce and chill. Break the lettuce into bite-sized pieces, toss with the prawns and arrange in a bowl. Pour the dressing over just before serving.

Serves 6–8

MEXICADO SALAD

3 medium-sized avocados, halved and stoned
⅓ cup mayonnaise (page 95)
1½ tablespoons lemon juice
¼ teaspoon Tabasco sauce
¼ teaspoon ground chillies
1 large clove garlic, crushed
salt
2 medium-sized tomatoes, peeled and chopped
6 shallots sliced
¾ cup chopped celery
1 small green capsicum, coarsely chopped
60 g black olives, stoned and chopped
2 rashers bacon, crisply cooked, or 2 tablespoons bacon chips
lettuce leaves

A cool crisp salad to serve with meat and seafood or alone as a first course.

Scoop the avocado flesh from the shells and mash or purée with the mayonnaise, lemon juice, Tabasco and ground chilli. Add the garlic and season to taste with salt. Fold the tomatoes, shallots, celery, capsicum and olives through the sauce and chill. Pile the salad into the avocado shells or over crisp lettuce leaves. Serve lightly sprinkled with crumbled bacon or bacon chips.

Serves 6

AVOCADO BAGRATION SALAD

400 g can artichoke hearts, drained and halved
2 stalks celery, thinly sliced
1½ cups cooked macaroni
1 large avocado, peeled, stoned and cubed
1 tablespoon lemon juice
salt
black pepper
1 cup mayonnaise (page 95)
1½ tablespoons tomato paste
3 tablespoons cream
100 g sliced tongue or ham, cut into strips
2 hard-boiled eggs
2 tablespoons finely chopped parsley

Toss the artichokes, celery, macaroni, avocado and lemon juice together. Season with salt and pepper. Blend the mayonnaise, tomato paste and cream. Fold ¾ of the mayonnaise through the salad and pile the mixture, dome fashion, on a serving platter or individual lettuce cups. Garnish the salad with the tongue, or ham, and hard-boiled eggs. Spoon the remaining mayonnaise over the top and sprinkle with parsley.

Serves 6

TOMATO AND AVOCADO SALAD

½ cup vinaigrette dressing (page 94)
1 tablespoon chopped coriander or parsley
1 tablespoon cream
500 g firm ripe tomatoes, cut in wedges
4 spring onions, thinly sliced
2 avocados, peeled, stoned and cubed
1 sweet yellow chilli, seeded and sliced
lettuce leaves

Blend ⅓ cup of dressing with the coriander, or parsley, and cream. Put the tomatoes, onions, avocados and chilli in a bowl, add the dressing and turn the ingredients together until evenly coated. Chill thoroughly. Arrange the lettuce leaves in a serving bowl, sprinkle with the remaining vinaigrette. Arrange the chilled salad on top of the lettuce.

Serves 4–6

BEETROOT AND AVOCADO SALAD

2 medium-sized beetroot, approx. 300 g
1 avocado, peeled, stoned and diced
juice ½ lemon
salt
black pepper
1 tablespoon drained capers
2 teaspoons chopped fresh basil or parsley
2 tablespoons vinaigrette dressing (page 94)

Wash the beetroot and trim the leaves and roots. Plunge in boiling salted water and simmer for 2 minutes. Cool under cold running water. Peel and grate the beetroot. Turn the diced avocado in lemon juice, drain and add to the beetroot, fork together. Season the salad to taste, arrange in a bowl and sprinkle the capers over. Chill for 30 minutes. Moisten with vinaigrette just before serving.

Serves 4–6

CARROT AND AVOCADO SALAD

250 g carrots, coarsely grated
2 oranges
1 tablespoon lemon juice
3 teaspoons finely grated root ginger
¼ teaspoon castor sugar
2 avocados
6 anchovy fillets, chopped

Traditionally this salad is called Living Carrots and it certainly is a lively combination. Serve it as a first course or as an accompaniment to grilled meat.

Put the carrots into a bowl with the finely grated rind of 1 orange and the juice of both. Add the lemon juice, ginger, sugar and salt, mix thoroughly and refrigerate, covered, for 3–4 hours. Peel and stone the avocados, cut crossways in 1 cm slices. Fold the avocados and carrots together and top with the anchovies.

Serves 4–6

AVOCADO AND SNOW PEA SALAD

100–150 g snow peas
1 teaspoon dry mustard
1 teaspoon chopped parsley
1 teaspoon chopped fresh basil or mint
pinch celery seeds
1 tablespoon white wine vinegar
3 tablespoons olive oil
salt
pepper
1 avocado

Top and tail the peas, remove any coarse strings and leave them whole. Have ready a pan of salted, boiling water. Drop the peas into the water and boil for 2–3 minutes, or until crisply tender. Drain. While the peas are cooking blend mustard, herbs and celery seeds with the vinegar. Add the oil, blend thoroughly and season to taste. Pour the dressing over the hot peas and leave at room temperature until cold. Peel, stone and slice the avocado. Turn with the peas until coated in dressing. Chill before serving.

Serves 4–6

MUSHROOM AND AVOCADO SALAD

¾ cup natural yoghurt
2–3 teaspoons lemon juice
1 tablespoon bottled tomato sauce
salt
Cayenne pepper
125 g button mushrooms, thinly sliced
1 avocado, peeled, stoned and cubed
1½ tablespoons chopped chives

Blend the yoghurt, lemon juice and tomato sauce together. Season generously with salt and Cayenne. Put the remaining ingredients into a bowl, pour the dressing over and fork gently together until evenly coated. Chill for 2–3 hours before serving.

Serves 4–5

CRANBERRY AVOCADO SALAD

2 mignonette lettuce
210 g can cranberries, drained
2 small avocados
2 stalks celery, thinly sliced
2 teaspoons lemon juice
1 teaspoon castor sugar
⅓ cup cream
salt
black pepper
finely grated rind ½ lemon

Dry the lettuce very thoroughly, arrange in a salad bowl and scatter the cranberries over. Peel and stone the avocados. Reserve one half and slice the rest. Brush the avocado slices with cold water and add to the salad with the celery. Purée the reserved avocado, blend with lemon juice and cream. Season to taste with salt and pepper. Drizzle the sauce over the salad and sprinkle with lemon rind.

Serves 6

CLOVER SALAD

1 lettuce, shredded
125 g crumbly blue cheese, Roquefort or Danish
5 rindless rashers bacon, crisply cooked
500 g ripe tomatoes, peeled, seeded and chopped
2 medium-sized avocados, peeled and stoned
3 teaspoons lemon juice
¼ cup olive oil
2 tablespoons herb vinegar
salt
black pepper

This is a very pretty centrepiece arrangement more than a salad in the usual sense. Everyone helps themselves to each of the ingredients and anyone who is picky about something can leave it.

Spread the lettuce over a shallow platter. Crumble the cheese and arrange in a circle to form one part of the clover leaf. Crumble the bacon and make another circle, likewise the tomatoes. Cube or ball the avocados with a melon ball cutter, coat with lemon juice and arrange on the lettuce in a fourth circle. Chill. Before serving blend the oil and vinegar together, season to taste and sprinkle over the salad.

Serves 6

Avocado Mould, page 42
A light entrée with creamy texture and delicate spicing.

Overleaf
Avocado Danish Pastries, pages 84–87
Crescents, Windmills and Pinwheels of rich yeast pastry with avocado, nut and fruit filling.

SPINACH AND AVOCADO SALAD

2 tablespoons white wine vinegar
1 teaspoon salt
1/4 teaspoon black pepper
pinch sugar
2 dried red chillies
2 cloves garlic, coarsely chopped
1/2 cup olive or vegetable oil
1 bunch spinach
2 rashers bacon, crisply cooked
1 large avocado
6 white mushrooms, thinly sliced
1 canned pimiento, drained and sliced, or 1 ripe tomato, peeled, seeded and sliced

Silver beet, English spinach or dandelion greens can all be used in this rich dark salad which is very good with grilled meats.

Blend the vinegar, salt, pepper and sugar. Add the chillies, garlic and oil and stir well. Stand at room temperature for at least 1 hour. Wash the spinach and dry thoroughly, arrange in a salad bowl or on individual plates. Crumble the bacon. Peel, stone and slice the avocado crossways to form half circles. Carefully toss the bacon, avocado and mushrooms together, spread over the spinach. Top with strips of pimiento or tomato. Strain the dressing and shake or whisk together until lightly thickened. Drizzle over the salad before serving.

Serves 6

NEW MEXICO SALAD

1 lettuce
2 medium-sized ripe tomatoes, sliced and seeded
2 sweet chilli peppers, seeded and coarsely chopped
100 g stoned olives, green or black
1 avocado, peeled, stoned and mashed
1/4 cup light sour cream
2 tablespoons olive oil
2 tablespoons lemon juice
1/8 teaspoon ground chillies
salt
1/2 cup grated Cheddar cheese
1 cup lightly crushed corn chips

Dry the lettuce thoroughly, break into bite-sized pieces and toss with the tomatoes, chillies and olives. Arrange in a salad bowl and chill. Blend the avocado, sour cream, oil and lemon juice, add the ground chillies and salt to taste. Drizzle the sauce over the salad and sprinkle with the grated cheese and corn chips.

Serves 6

Crab and Avocado Fusilli, page 62
A light but substantial pasta salad to serve as an entrée or luncheon.

RADICCHIO AND AVOCADO SALAD

2 heads radicchio
2 thick slices fresh pineapple, cut in chunks
1 large avocado
2 pickled hot chillies, seeded and finely chopped
1 clove garlic, crushed
1 tablespoon lemon juice
3 tablespoons olive oil
salt
black pepper
pinch castor sugar

This bittersweet salad has an underlying touch of fire and is very good with cold fish and white meats.

Dry the radicchio thoroughly and break into bite-sized pieces. If you cannot buy radicchio substitute 2 heads of Belgian endive. Arrange the radicchio in a bowl with the pineapple. Peel, stone and slice the avocado, arrange in the bowl. Blend the chillies, garlic and lemon juice, add the oil and season with salt, pepper and sugar. Shake thoroughly together and drizzle over the salad.

Serves 4–6

CAULIFLOWER AND AVOCADO SALAD

1 small or ½ large cauliflower, broken into flowerets
salt
3 tablespoons white wine vinegar
1 teaspoon olive oil
¼ teaspoon white pepper
pinch ground mace
2 medium-sized avocados, peeled, stoned and puréed
2 teaspoons lemon juice
3 cups ground almonds
4 shallots, chopped
4 radishes, chopped

A salad to serve hot or cold with meat, poultry or seafood.

Cook the cauliflowerets in salted, boiling water until just tender. Drain and arrange in a serving dish. While the cauliflower is cooking blend the vinegar, oil, pepper and mace together, pour the dressing over the hot cauliflower. Blend the avocado, lemon juice and almonds. Spoon the purée over the cauliflower and sprinkle with the chopped shallots and radishes.

Serves 6

APPLE AND AVOCADO SALAD

finely grated rind 1 lemon
3 tablespoons lemon juice
1 teaspoon castor sugar
3 tablespoons olive oil
salt
black pepper
1 red apple
1 green apple
1 large avocado
lettuce

Blend the lemon rind and juice with the sugar, add the oil and season to taste. Peel, stone and slice the avocado crossways and put the slices into the dressing. Core and thinly slice the unpeeled apples, turn them in the dressing with the avocado, and chill. Break the lettuce into bite-sized pieces and place in a salad bowl. Tip the avocado mixture into the bowl and fork gently with the lettuce.

Serves 4

AVOCADO CHAPON SALAD

4 tablespoons olive oil
2 large cloves garlic, crushed
salt
black pepper
8 slices French bread
2 avocados
3 tablespoons vinaigrette dressing (page 94)
1 bunch watercress

This is a marvellous salad to serve with grills and particularly barbecues.

Blend the olive oil and garlic and brush lightly over each side of the sliced bread. Season the bread with salt and lots of black pepper. Peel and stone the avocados, cut into thick slices and brush with the vinaigrette. Arrange the bread, avocados and watercress in a bowl and sprinkle with the remaining vinaigrette.

Serves 4, or 8 with other salads

PAWPAW AND AVOCADO SALAD

1 small ripe pawpaw
1 mignonette or cos lettuce
1 avocado
2 tablespoons lemon juice
3 tablespoons olive oil
1 tablespoon finely chopped mint
salt
black pepper

Cut the pawpaw into cubes or ball with a melon baller. Arrange the outer leaves of the lettuce in a shallow bowl. Shred the remaining lettuce, toss with the pawpaw. Peel, stone and slice the avocado, brush the slices with a little lemon juice and fold into the pawpaw. Pile the salad on top of the lettuce leaves and chill. Blend the lemon juice, oil and mint, season to taste and pour the dressing over the salad just before serving.

Serves 4–6

Desserts, Cakes, and Pastries

Few people consider avocados when planning desserts and making pastries, but their very texture allows them to be turned into a delicate cold soufflé, an iced parfait or a moist and unusual cake.

If you are in doubt, first try avocados at their simplest—blended with a little lemon juice and sugar. They are reminiscent of all things tropical, hinting of mango, banana and passionfruit all in one package.

COLD AVOCADO CITRUS SOUFFLÉ

4 eggs, separated
1 cup castor sugar
finely grated rind 1 lemon
juice 2 lemons
5 teaspoons gelatine
¼ cup cold water
1 medium-sized avocado, peeled, stoned and puréed
¾ cup cream, stiffly whipped
additional cream for piping
grated chocolate

Always a pretty dessert, yet simple to make. Serve alone or with a few fresh berries.

Tie a band of non-stick or lightly oiled greaseproof paper around a 15 or 16 cm soufflé dish. The collar should stand about 6 cm above the rim of the dish. Set the dish aside. Put the egg yolks and sugar in the top of a double boiler, or a basin set over gently simmering water. Beat the mixture until it is pale and thick enough to leave a ribbon track on itself for a few seconds. Remove from the heat, add the lemon rind and juice and continue beating until the mixture is almost cold. Sprinkle the gelatine over cold water and dissolve over low heat. Strain the gelatine and stir into the egg mixture. Add the avocado purée and stir until just blended. Fold in the whipped cream. Beat the egg whites until stiff and fold into the cream mixture. Spoon into the prepared soufflé dish and level the top. Refrigerate for at least 6 hours or overnight. To serve, carefully remove the paper and decorate the top with rosettes of cream and the grated chocolate.

Serves 6

APRICOT AND AVOCADO MOUSSE

250 g dried apricots
⅓ cup castor sugar
1 cup water
finely grated rind and juice 1 lemon
1 large avocado
1 cup cream, stiffly whipped

Put the apricots, ¼ cup of the sugar, water and lemon rind in a small pan. Bring slowly to the boil, cover and simmer gently for 15–20 minutes until the apricots are plump and softened, but not mushy. Reserve 6 of the cooked apricots. Purée the remaining apricots and their juice, add more sugar or lemon juice to taste. Chill. Peel, stone and mash the avocado, add the remaining sugar and lemon juice to taste. Chop the reserved apricots coarsely, fold through the avocado mixture with half of the whipped cream. Blend the apricot purée with the remaining cream. Spoon the two mixtures alternately into tall glasses. Chill before serving.

AVOCADO PRUNE MOUSSE
Substitute 250 g stoned dessert prunes for the apricots and prepare as above.

Serves 4–6

AVOCADO ICE-CREAM

2 medium-sized avocados
3 eggs, separated
¼ cup orange juice, or ¼ cup peach or apricot nectar
1 tablespoon lemon juice
⅓ cup castor sugar
300 ml carton cream, stiffly whipped
¼ cup chopped unsalted nuts, optional

Peel, stone and purée the avocados, add the egg yolks, one at a time, and mix lightly through the purée. Add the fruit juices and beat thoroughly together until the eggs and juice are well blended. Set aside. Beat the egg whites until stiff peaks form, then whisk in the sugar a tablespoon at a time. Lightly fold the whipped cream and avocado mixtures together and then fold into the egg whites with the nuts. Pour the mixture into freezer trays, cover loosely and freeze for at least 4 hours, or until firm.

Serves 6

AVOCADO PARFAIT

6 tablespoons sifted icing sugar
3 egg yolks
2 medium-sized avocados, peeled, stoned and puréed
3 teaspoons castor sugar
juice 1 lemon
½ cup cream, whipped

A delicious frozen dessert with a tropical flavour.

Beat the egg yolks and icing sugar together in the top of a double saucepan. Set the pan over the base containing water that is barely simmering. Beat the egg mixture until it is warm but not hot. Remove the pan from the heat and continue beating until the mixture is almost cold. Sieve the avocado purée to remove any fibres, add the castor sugar and lemon juice. Fold the avocado mixture and whipped cream into the egg mixture, pour into a freezer tray and freeze for 2–3 hours.

Serves 4–5

AVOCADO MOCHA CREAM TARTLETS

2 cups flour
pinch salt
150 g butter
cold water
3 egg yolks
1 tablespoon unsweetened cocoa
2 teaspoons instant coffee powder
¼ cup strong black coffee
¼ cup castor sugar
1 small avocado
24 pecan or walnut halves

Crisp short pastry cups filled with a delicious blend of mocha and avocado cream.

Sift the flour and salt together, rub in the butter and mix to a dough with cold water. Collect the pastry into a ball, cover closely with plastic film and refrigerate for 20 minutes or more. Preheat the oven to 200°C. Roll the pastry thinly and cut into circles with a 7.5 cm cutter. Line 6 cm tartlet tins with the pastry and prick the pastry with a fork. Press small circles of foil into the tins to line the cups. Bake for 10 minutes. Remove the foil and bake for a further 5 minutes or until the pastry is crisp and golden. Cool. Beat the egg yolks, cocoa and coffee powder together until thick and creamy. Set aside. Boil the black coffee and sugar together until a thread forms when the syrup is dripped from a spoon. Beating constantly pour the coffee syrup onto the egg mixture. Continue beating until the mixture is almost cold. Peel, stone and mash the avocado, beat into the mocha cream. Chill. Spoon the avocado cream into the cold pastry cases, level the tops and press a pecan or walnut on each.

Makes 24

AVOCADO SORBET

1 large avocado, peeled and stoned
½ cup cream, whipped
finely grated rind 1 orange
1 cup orange juice
1½–2 tablespoons lemon juice
2½ tablespoons honey

Mash the avocado, blend with the cream until smooth. Add the orange rind, juices and honey. Pour into a tray and freeze for 2 hours. Stir the sorbet to break up any ice crystals and freeze until firm but not hard, approximately 2 hours.

Serves 4–5

MEDITERRANEAN FRUIT SALAD

3 oranges, peeled and segmented
2 grapefruit, peeled and segmented
2 avocados, peeled and stoned
juice 1 lemon
2–3 tablespoons castor sugar
200 g cottage cheese
pulp 3 passionfruit

Carefully cut the membrane from the orange and grapefruit segments. Slice the avocados lengthways, brush the slices with lemon juice. Arrange the fruit alternately around a platter and drizzle with the remaining lemon juice. Sprinkle sugar over the citrus and avocado slices. Form the cheese into a ball and centre on the dish. Pour a little passionfruit over the cheese and the rest over the fruit. Chill before serving.

Serves 6

AUSTRALIAN FRUIT SALAD

2 avocados, peeled and stoned
2 dessert apples, cored and sliced
1 banana, peeled and sliced
2 oranges, peeled and segmented
1 grapefruit, peeled and segmented
1 cup pineapple cubes, fresh or canned
⅓ cup unsalted nuts
juice and seeds 2 passionfruit
⅛ teaspoon black pepper
1 tablespoon mayonnaise
¼ cup cream

Quarter and slice the avocados and layer in a bowl with the apples and banana. Remove any tough membrane from the orange and grapefruit segments and halve the segments if large. Save any juice from the citrus fruits and add to the bowl with the fruit. Add the pineapple, nuts, passionfruit and pepper without disturbing the fruit layering. Cover the bowl and leave at room temperature for at least an hour for the juice to run. Stir the mayonnaise and cream together, pour over the fruit and carefully mix the salad together until all the fruit is lightly coated with the blend of fruit juice and cream. Chill thoroughly before serving.

Serves 6–8

AVOCADO BERRY NEST

4 egg whites
¼ teaspoon cream of tartar
¾ cup castor sugar
1 avocado, peeled, stoned and thinly sliced
250 g fresh berry fruit, e.g. blackcurrants, raspberries
additional sugar
1 cup cream, stiffly whipped

A nest of meringue lined with avocado and crowned with a blend of berries and cream.

Preheat the oven to 120°C and line the base of a 21 cm spring form cake tin with non-stick or lightly oiled greaseproof paper. Beat the egg whites and cream of tartar until stiff peaks form. Add ¼ cup of the castor sugar, beat until glossy. Fold in the remaining castor sugar. Tip the meringue mixture into the lined cake tin and spread evenly over the base. Make a shallow depression in the centre of the meringue to form the nest. Bake 1½–2 hours until the outside of the meringue is crisp. Carefully remove from the cake tin and cool on a serving platter. Reserve 2 or 3 slices of avocado to garnish, brush these slices with cold water and set aside. Line the meringue with the remaining avocado. Sweeten the berries to taste and fold into the cream. Swirl the cream mixture over the avocado, garnish and chill before serving.

Serves 6

ORANGE AND AVOCADO COMPÔTE

3 large oranges
½ cup castor sugar
¼ cup water
2 tablespoons lemon juice
1 large avocado
3 tablespoons orange liqueur
¾ cup cream
½ teaspoon vanilla essence
sifted icing sugar
1 tablespoon flaked almonds, lightly toasted, optional

Pare the thinnest possible rind from 1 orange. Cut the rind in fine julienne strips. Dissolve the sugar in water and lemon juice, add the rind and boil rapidly for 2 minutes. Set aside. Peel and segment the oranges, remove all white pith and membrane. Peel and stone the avocado and slice crossways. Layer the fruit into a serving bowl or individual glasses. Combine the syrup and liqueur, spoon over the fruit and marinate for 3 hours in the refrigerator. Whip the cream and vanilla, sweeten slightly with sugar, and spoon over the fruit. Serve lightly sprinkled with almonds if liked.

Serves 4–6

*Avocado in its many guises. Choux pastry with a zesty avocado cream comprise **Piquant Avocado Puffs, page 15**. Add colour and texture to **Pan Braised Veal Cutlets, page 45**. A blend of complementary flavours in **Pawpaw and Avocado Salad, page 73**. **Refreshing Avocado Soda, page 90** and the delicious **Avocado Teabread, page 88**.*

AVOCADO AND STRAWBERRY MILLEFEUILLE

375 g puff pastry
1 large avocado
juice ½ lemon
3 tablespoons sifted icing sugar
2 punnets strawberries, hulled
2 tablespoons fresh orange juice
2 tablespoons orange liqueur
300 ml cream, whipped

Preheat the oven to 200°C. Roll the pastry thinly, 3 to 4 cm. Cut into 3 equal sized rectangles and place on baking trays. Bake for 20–30 minutes until well puffed and golden. Cool. Peel, stone and quarter the avocado, cut crossways into small fans. Add the lemon juice and 3 teaspoons of the icing sugar to the avocado and set aside. Slice half of the strawberries, sprinkle with 2 teaspoons sugar and stand until the juice runs. Purée the remaining strawberries and blend with the orange juice and the liqueur. Strain the sauce and chill. To assemble the millefeuille drain the avocado and strawberries, keeping the fruit separate but reserving the juice. Fold the avocado through half the cream and layer onto a pastry sheet. Cover with pastry. Fold the sliced strawberries into the remaining cream, layer onto the second pastry sheet and top with the third. Dust the top lightly with icing sugar. Blend the reserved juices into the sauce and serve with the millefeuille.

Serves 6

AVOCADO RUM PIE

1 baked 23 cm pastry shell (page 84)
4 eggs, separated
2 teaspoons butter
⅛ teaspoon mixed spice
⅓–½ cup castor sugar
juice ½ lemon
3 teaspoons gelatine
¼ cup light rum
1 medium-sized avocado, peeled, stoned and puréed
2 thin slices lemon, to garnish

Put the egg yolks, butter, mixed spice, ⅓ cup of the sugar and lemon juice in the top of a double boiler or a basin set over gently simmering water. Stir together until hot but not boiling, sprinkle the gelatine over the rum, stir over low heat until the gelatine has melted. Strain the gelatine into the egg mixture and blend thoroughly. Add the avocado purée, blend and cool to room temperature. Beat the egg whites until stiff peaks form. Add the remaining sugar and beat well. Fold the egg whites into the avocado mixture, pour into the prepared pastry shell and chill before serving garnished with lemon.

Serves 6

Cold Avocado Citrus Soufflé, page 74
A pretty, cooling dessert to serve alone or with fresh berries.

AVOCADO NUT GÂTEAU

125 g hazelnuts
½ cup hot milk
90 g butter
90 g icing sugar
2 egg yolks, lightly beaten
1 medium-sized avocado, peeled, stoned and mashed
1 cup cold milk
2 tablespoons cherry brandy
red food colouring
500 g savoiardi biscuits
¾ cup cream, whipped

This is an unbaked party cake of extravagant nature. Make it in a spring-form tin and weight it overnight.

Preheat the oven to 210°C. Spread the nuts on a baking tray and toast in the oven for 10 minutes. Rub the skins from the nuts on a dry teatowel and grind the nuts finely. You can use preground hazelnut meal but the flavour is not as good from untoasted nuts. Put the nuts into a small bowl, pour the hot milk over and leave until cold. Cream the butter and sugar until fluffy, add the egg yolks and avocado and beat well. Combine the avocado and nut mixtures and blend without beating. Set aside. Lightly butter a 21 cm cake tin. Combine the milk and cherry brandy in a shallow dish. Add enough red colouring to shade the biscuits a good peach colour (dip one in to try). Dip the savoiardi, one at a time and very briefly, into the milk mixture. Line the base of the cake tin with the dipped biscuits. Cover most of the base with whole biscuits and fill in the gaps with pieces. Cover with a layer of the avocado mixture then another layer of soaked savoiardi. Repeat the layering, finishing with biscuits. Cover the top of the cake with a circle of non-stick paper or lightly buttered foil. Place a flat plate or cake tin base directly onto the paper and weight it down, some heavy cans will do. Stand the cake tin on a plate and refrigerate, with the weights, overnight or at least for several hours. Carefully remove the cake from the tin and place on a serving dish. Cut the remaining savoiardi to the height of the cake and stick around the edge with whipped cream. Pipe or coat the top of the cake with the remaining cream.

Serves 6–8

CARIBBEAN CREAM

2 avocados, peeled and stoned
2 tablespoons lime or lemon juice
¼ cup rum
1 cup cream, stiffly whipped
¼ cup castor sugar
pinch ground cinnamon
freshly grated nutmeg
savoiardi biscuits for serving

Purée the avocados with the lime or lemon juice and the rum. Blend the cream, sugar and cinnamon, fold into the avocado purée. Spoon the mixture into serving dishes, sprinkle the tops lightly with nutmeg and chill before serving with the biscuits.

Serves 4–5

AVOCADO CHIFFON TART

16 wholemeal biscuits, crushed
60 g ground hazelnuts
½ cup castor sugar
4 tablespoons melted butter
1 tablespoon gelatine
1 cup cold water
3 eggs, separated
¾ cup cold milk
⅓ cup castor sugar
1 medium-sized avocado, peeled, stoned and mashed
½ cup strained orange juice
½ cup strained lemon juice
whipped cream for serving

Preheat the oven to 150°C. Lightly oil a 23 cm, loose bottomed flan tin. Combine the crushed crumbs, nuts and 2 tablespoons of the sugar. Add the melted butter. Press the mixture evenly over the sides and base of the flan tin. Bake for 20 minutes and cool. Sprinkle the gelatine over the cold water and leave to soak. Put the egg yolks, milk and 2 tablespoons of sugar in the top of a double boiler or a basin set over simmering water. Stir the custard until lightly thickened 4–5 minutes. Strain the gelatine mixture into the custard and continue stirring until dissolved. Remove the custard from the heat, add the avocado and fruit juices and beat with a whisk or electric beater until the mixture has cooled to lukewarm. Refrigerate until cold. Whisk the egg whites until stiff peaks form, add the remaining sugar and beat until the egg whites are glossy. Fold into the avocado mixture and pour into the cooled tart. Chill for 2 hours or until firm. Serve with whipped cream.

Serves 6

CHERRY AVOCADO FLAN

1 cup flour
pinch salt
2 tablespoons sifted icing sugar
60 g almond meal
125 g butter
1 tablespoon iced water
4 drops almond essence
125 g ricotta cheese
finely grated rind and juice 1 lemon
1 large avocado, peeled, stoned and sliced
1 cup Morello cherries, stoned
½ cup cherry juice
1½ teaspoons potato flour or arrowroot
castor sugar

Sift the flour, salt and 1 tablespoon of the icing sugar together. Add the almond meal, mix well. Rub in the butter and mix to a soft dough with the water and essence. Cover closely with plastic film and refrigerate for 1 hour. Roll the pastry thinly and line a 23 cm flan tin. Trim the edges and prick the base of the pastry with a fork. Line the flan with foil, pressing it well into the corners. Chill for 15 minutes to firm the pastry. Preheat the oven to 200°C. Bake the flan for 15 minutes, remove the foil and bake the flan for another 5 minutes, or until crisp. Cool. Blend the cheese, lemon rind and remaining icing sugar. Spread evenly over the base of the flan. Brush the sliced avocado with a little of the lemon juice and set aside. Blend the cherry juice, lemon juice and potato flour, stir over low heat until thickened and clear. Sweeten to taste and cool. Arrange the avocado slices in the flan, radiating from the centre. Fill the spaces between the avocado with drifts of cherries. Coat the fruit with the cherry glaze and chill before serving.

Serves 6

SHORTCRUST PASTRY

2 cups flour
pinch salt
2 teaspoons icing sugar
125 g butter
1 egg yolk
2 teaspoons lemon juice
iced water

Omit the icing sugar for savoury flans. Sift flour, salt and sugar together. Rub the butter in with fingertips until it resembles fine breadcrumbs. Mix to a fairly stiff dough with the egg yolk, lemon juice and about 2 tablespoons of iced water. Form the dough into a ball, cover closely with plastic film and refrigerate 1 hour. Use as directed in a particular recipe.

To bake the pastry blind (empty), roll the chilled pastry thinly and line a 23 cm flan tin or ring. Trim the pastry edges and prick the base with a fork. Line the pastry with foil, pressing it well into the corners. Chill for 30 minutes. Preheat the oven to 190°C, bake the flan for 20 minutes. Remove the foil and bake 5–10 minutes longer until crisp and golden. Cool before filling.

Sufficient for 1×23 cm flan case
Makes 24

AVOCADO DANISH PASTRIES

For some reason the Danes call their famous yeast puff pastry Wienerbrød or Viennese bread, but whatever you call it, the light, buttery pastry is delicious at any time of day. The recipe I have given for the basic dough makes 20 large pastries. The preparation is a little time consuming, although this is compensated by using avocado as the filling, with no need for custards or glazing. The dough freezes very well and it is worthwhile to make a batch, bake some and freeze some for later use.

Danish Pastry

280 g butter
3 cups flour
pinch salt
30 g fresh yeast, or scant 15 g dried yeast
2 tablespoons castor sugar
1 cup lukewarm milk
1 egg, lightly beaten

Melt one-quarter cup of the butter over low heat. Set aside and cool. Sift the flour and salt into a mixing bowl. Cream the yeast with the sugar until it liquefies, add the milk and the melted butter, blend thoroughly and add the egg. Pour the yeast mixture into the flour and mix to a smooth dough. Leave the dough in the bowl, cover and leave at room temperature until the dough has doubled in volume, approximately 1 hour. Punch the dough down, turn onto a lightly floured board and knead lightly. Roll the dough to a large oblong. Divide the remaining butter in small pieces and dot two-thirds of the dough with half of the butter. Fold the dough in three, pressing the unbuttered portion of the pastry over one-half of the buttered piece. Give the pastry a one-quarter turn and roll again to an oblong. Dot the dough with the remaining butter, fold into 3 and leave for 15 minutes. Roll and fold the pastry twice more and leave at room temperature for 15 minutes after the final folding. Chill the dough for 10 minutes. Cut the dough in 3 and roll each to a 30 × 20 cm rectangle. Cut and fill for Windmills, Pinwheels or Crescents (see pages 86 and 87).

Note If you wish to freeze a portion of the dough, wrap for the freezer in an airtight pack and label clearly. Storage time is 12 weeks. To defrost, thaw in loose wrapping in the refrigerator, prove the defrosted dough at room temperature for 30 minutes and chill again for 10 minutes before the final rolling.

CHOUX PASTRY

90 g butter
pinch salt
⅓ cup water
1 tablespoon castor sugar (for dessert choux, omit for savoury)
1 scant cup plain flour
3 eggs, well beaten

Put the butter, salt, sugar if using, and water into a saucepan and bring slowly to the boil. Boil briefly and remove from the heat. Tip all the flour into the mixture and beat together until it leaves the sides of the pan. Beat the eggs, one at a time, add to the mixture and beat in. You will have to cut the egg in to begin with because it will be slipping and sliding all over the place. As you beat the paste it will become smooth. Repeat with the remaining eggs. Cover the pastry and allow to become completely cold at room temperature before using. Use as directed in a particular recipe.

Makes 24 small puffs or a 23 cm pie

Avocado Danish Pinwheels

⅓ quantity Danish Pastry (page 85)
1 small avocado, mashed
½ cup ground almonds
finely grated rind ½ lemon
lemon juice
1 tablespoon castor sugar
2 tablespoons seedless raisins
1 lightly beaten egg
½ cup sifted icing sugar

Chill the pastry and lightly oil a baking tray. Blend the avocado, almonds, lemon rind, 3 teaspoons lemon juice and the castor sugar together, set aside. Roll the pastry to a 30 × 20 cm rectangle. Spread the avocado mixture evenly over the dough and sprinkle with the raisins. Roll the dough, from the short side, into a thick roll. Cut in 8 thick slices and place the pinwheels, cut side down, on the baking tray. Flatten slightly with the side of a knife, cover and prove in a warm place for 20 minutes. Preheat the oven to 220°C. Glaze the pinwheels with a little beaten egg and bake for 10–12 minutes. Cool on a rack. Blend the icing sugar with enough strained lemon juice to form a light coating consistency. Drizzle a little icing over the pastries while they are still warm.

Makes 8 pastries

Avocado Danish Windmills

⅓ quantity Danish Pastry (page 85)
1 small avocado, peeled, stoned and mashed
¼ cup chopped unsalted nuts
3 dried apricot halves, finely chopped
lemon juice
3 teaspoons castor sugar
lightly beaten egg
½ cup sifted icing sugar

Lightly oil a baking tray. Roll the pastry into a 30 × 20 cm rectangle and cut into 6 squares. On each square make a diagonal cut from each corner to within 2 cm of the centre. Blend the avocado, nuts and apricots with lemon juice to taste, about 3 teaspoons, and the castor sugar. Place 2 teaspoons of the mixture on the centre of each square, fold alternate corners over the filling and press lightly together. Put the pastries on the baking tray, cover, and leave in a warm place for 20 minutes. Preheat the oven to 220°C. Brush the pastries lightly with egg and bake for 15–16 minutes. Cool on racks. Blend the icing sugar with enough lemon juice to form a coating consistency and drizzle a little over each pastry while still warm.

Makes 6 pastries

Avocado Danish Crescents

- 1/3 quantity Danish Pastry (page 85)
- 1 small avocado, peeled, stoned and mashed
- 1/4 cup cottage cheese
- finely grated rind and juice 1/2 lemon
- 1/4 cup chopped mixed peel or sultanas
- castor sugar
- 1 beaten egg
- 1/2 cup sifted icing sugar

Lightly oil two baking sheets and set aside. Roll the pastry to a 30 × 20 cm rectangle and cut into 6 squares. Cut each square diagonally in half to form a triangle. Blend the avocado, cheese, lemon rind and chopped peel or sultanas, add lemon juice and castor sugar to taste. Place a spoonful of the filling in the centre of each triangle and spread slightly over the dough. Roll each from the long edge, moisten the point with a spot of egg to fasten and curve each roll into a crescent. Place the crescents, well spaced on the baking trays, cover, and leave in a warm place for 20 minutes. Preheat the oven to 220°C. Brush the crescents lightly with egg and bake for 14–15 minutes. Cool slightly on racks and dust with icing sugar while still warm.

Makes 12

SHORTCAKES WITH AVOCADO

- 2 cups plain flour
- 2 teaspoons baking powder
- 60 g butter
- castor sugar
- 1 egg, lightly beaten
- 4–5 tablespoons milk
- 2 medium-sized avocados
- 3 tablespoons lemon juice
- whipped cream for serving

Preheat oven to 230°C. Lightly grease a baking sheet. Sift flour and baking powder together. Rub in the butter and add 1½ tablespoons castor sugar. Mix to a fairly stiff dough with the egg and milk. Turn the dough onto a lightly floured board, roll to thickness of 1.5 cm. Cut into rounds using a plain 5 cm cutter. Place on the baking sheet and bake for 12 minutes or until the shortcakes are well raised and golden. Split the shortcakes through the centre while still warm and cool on a rack. Shortly before serving prepare the filling. Peel and stone the avocados. Mash 1 with a fork, and cut the other into small dice. Fold the mashed and diced avocados together with the lemon juice and sugar to taste. Pile the filling between the split shortcakes, dust the tops lightly with sugar and serve with a little whipped cream.

Makes 14–16

AVOCADO SCONES

2 cups self-raising flour
1 teaspoon baking powder
pinch salt
3 tablespoons butter
1 tablespoon castor sugar
1 egg, lightly beaten
1 small avocado, peeled, stoned and puréed
1 tablespoon fresh or sour cream
1 tablespoon milk for glazing

Serve these light, rich scones with whipped cream and jam or cream cheese smoothly blended with strained passionfruit pulp.

Preheat the oven to 210°C and lightly oil a baking tray. Sift the flour, baking powder and salt into a mixing bowl. Rub in the butter and add the sugar. Add the egg, avocado and cream and blend thoroughly to form a soft dough. Turn onto a lightly floured board and knead lightly until smooth. Roll to a 2 cm thickness and cut with a plain, floured 4.5 cm cutter. Place the scones on the baking tray, brush the tops with milk and bake for 9–10 minutes.

Makes 16

AVOCADO TEABREAD

1 cup flour
1 teaspoon ground cinnamon
1 teaspoon baking powder
¼ teaspoon salt
pinch black pepper
2 eggs
1 cup castor sugar
¼ cup corn or safflower oil
⅓ cup sultanas
¾ cup coarsely chopped walnuts
1 large avocado, peeled, stoned and mashed
1½ tablespoons lemon juice
¼ cup sifted icing sugar

This unusual and moist teabread keeps well for several days. It can be varied by replacing the sultanas with equal quantities of chopped crystallised ginger and mixed peel.

Grease and flour a 25×12×6 cm loaf tin and preheat the oven to 190°C. Sift the flour, cinnamon, baking powder, salt and pepper together and set aside. Beat the eggs, sugar and oil until light and fluffy. Add the sultanas, ½ cup of the nuts, the avocado and 3 teaspoons lemon juice, blend thoroughly without beating. Fold the sifted flour into the avocado mixture and pour into the prepared tin. Level the top and bake 55–60 minutes or until a cake tester comes out clean. Cool for 2 minutes in the tin, turn out and finish cooling on a rack. Blend the icing sugar with enough lemon juice to form a stiff icing, spread along the top of the teabread and press the remaining nuts over.

AVOCADO HARVEST CAKE

2 cups flour
3 teaspoons ground cinnamon
1 teaspoon allspice
½ teaspoon salt
1½ teaspoons bicarbonate of soda
185 g butter
2 cups castor sugar
3 eggs
2 medium-sized avocados, peeled, stoned and puréed
¾ cup buttermilk
2 teaspoons vanilla essence
½ cup chopped walnuts or pecan nuts
¾ cup seedless raisins

This is a spicy cake, again moist, as avocado cakes tend to be. The quantity given makes two cakes but they do freeze well.

Preheat the oven to 180°C. Grease and flour 2 loaf tins, 25×12×6 cm. Sift the dry ingredients together and set aside. Beat the butter until creamy, add the sugar and beat until light and fluffy. Beat in the eggs, one at a time. Fold the sifted flour into the egg mixture. Add the remaining ingredients and blend well without beating. Divide the mixture between the loaf tins and bake for 55–60 minutes or until a cake tester comes out clean. Cool on racks before slicing.

AVOCADO CAKE

1¼ cups flour
½ teaspoon salt
1⅓ cups castor sugar
125 g butter
2 eggs
1 large avocado, peeled, stoned and mashed
1½ teaspoons mixed spice
½ teaspoon bicarbonate of soda
⅓ cup buttermilk
½ cup chopped dates
¼ cup seedless raisins, chopped
½ cup coarsely chopped walnuts
whipped cream for serving, optional

Preheat the oven to 150°C. Grease and flour a 21 cm cake tin. Sift the flour and salt together and set aside. Cream the sugar and butter together until light in colour and fluffy. Beat in the eggs and avocado. Add the spice and bicarbonate of soda and beat again for a few seconds. Add the buttermilk, fruit and nuts and mix well. Fold in the flour. Spread the mixture in the cake tin, level the top and bake for 50–55 minutes or until a cake tester comes out clean. Cool on a cake rack before serving.

Drinks

If you enjoy a Bloody Mary you will certainly like the avocado drinks, cool and refreshing with just a little kick. And children who will not touch avocados certainly love the Avocado Soda. Incidentally, a very good hangover cure is vitamin B and avocados are very high in this particular vitamin.

AVOCADO SODA

1 medium-sized avocado, peeled and stoned
juice 1 large lemon
2 tablespoons castor sugar
1.25 litre bottle lemonade, chilled
250 g vanilla ice-cream
mint leaves for serving

And a long cool drink for children, of all ages! Much better than a milk shake and much better for you.

Purée the avocado with the lemon juice, sugar and 2 cups of the lemonade. Chill the avocado purée until ready to serve. Pour the purée into 6 tall, chilled glasses, stir in the remaining lemonade and top with a scoop of ice-cream. Serve garnished with mint leaves.

AVOCADO MARGARITAS

½ small avocado
¼ cup lemon juice
2 cups crushed ice
¾ cup tequila
¼ cup triple sec or Grand Marnier
Tabasco sauce

Purée the avocado with the lemon juice. Add the ice, tequila and triple sec, stir well and add Tabasco to taste. Serve in chilled, salt rimmed glasses.

Serves 4

AVOCADO SMOOTHIE

1 large avocado, peeled and stoned
250 g vanilla ice-cream
3 cups natural yoghurt, or milk
¾ teaspoon orange flower water, or 2–3 drops orange essence

Purée the avocado in a blender or food processor. Add the ice-cream and blend until smooth. Gradually add the yoghurt or milk (or equal quantities of each). Finally blend in the orange flower water or essence to taste. Serve in chilled glasses.

Serves 4–6

AVOCADO FROSTY

2 × 185 g cans frozen orange concentrate, unthawed
1 cup cold water
1 cup rum
4 tablespoons lemon juice
1 medium-sized avocado, peeled, stoned and cubed
ice cubes and lemon twists for serving

Put all the ingredients, except the ice cubes and lemon twists, in a blender or food processor. Blend briefly until smooth. Pour over ice cubes in chilled glasses and garnish with the lemon twists.

Serves 4–6

GREEN VELVET

1 large avocado, peeled and stoned
1 teaspoon very finely grated lemon rind
¼ cup lemon juice
2 cups chilled pineapple juice
1 cup gin
2 cups crushed ice
thin lemon slices to garnish

Purée the avocado with the lemon rind, fruit juices and gin. Stir in the ice and serve in chilled glasses with a lemon slice.

Serves 6–8

AVOCADO EGGNOG

4 cups milk
1 cup castor sugar
½ teaspoon, or more, ground allspice
¾ cup brandy, optional
4 egg yolks
1 small avocado
fine strips orange peel to garnish

Blend milk, sugar and spice in a large, heavy saucepan, stir over moderate heat until the sugar has dissolved. Bring to a rolling boil and remove from the heat. Set aside for several minutes until a crinkled skin forms on the surface. Beat the egg yolks until thick and pale in colour. Peel, stone and purée the avocado and blend smoothly with the egg yolks. Remove and discard the skin from the milk and stir in the brandy, if liked. Whisk the avocado mixture into the hot milk and chill thoroughly before serving garnished with thin slivers of orange peel.

Serves 4–8

Sauces and Basics

Avocado sauces are easy to prepare and quickly add a touch of luxury to a very simple meal.

AVOCADO TARTARE

1 small onion, finely chopped
3 teaspoons drained capers, chopped
4 cm cucumber, peeled, seeded and chopped
1 small avocado, peeled, stoned and mashed
¼ cup sour cream
salt
black pepper

This is one of those all things to all people mixtures. The simplest possible last minute dip, served with crisps, corn chips or crackers. A delicious sauce with cold fish and a relish with cold meats, particularly roast beef.

Blend the onion, capers, cucumber and avocado together. If making a dip or a relish use heavy sour cream; use light sour cream for a sauce. Add the sour cream, blend with the avocado mixture and season to taste. The mixture can be prepared well ahead of time because it does not discolour rapidly.

Makes ¾ cup

SPICY AVOCADO SAUCE

¼ cup olive or vegetable oil
3 teaspoons red wine vinegar
½ teaspoon finely chopped hot chilli
1 teaspoon salt
½ teaspoon black pepper
1 small ripe tomato
1 small ripe avocado, peeled, stoned and mashed
2 teaspoons finely chopped capsicum
1 hard-boiled egg, chopped
2 teaspoons chopped fresh coriander or parsley

A good sauce to serve with grilled meats and fish and particularly to add oomph to a barbecue.

Blend the oil, vinegar, chilli, salt and pepper. Chop the tomato and add to the oil mixture with the remaining ingredients. Fold together until well blended. Cover and allow the flavour to develop at room temperature for 30 minutes before serving.

Makes 1¼ cups

MINTY AVOCADO SAUCE

1 small avocado, peeled, stoned and puréed
2 tablespoons lemon juice
½ teaspoon castor sugar
1 tablespoon finely chopped fresh mint
salt
white pepper
½ clove garlic, crushed, optional

Serve with roast lamb for a subtle accompaniment.

Blend the avocado purée, lemon juice, sugar and mint. Season to taste with salt and pepper and add garlic if liked. Stand at room temperature for 30 minutes to allow the flavours to develop.

Makes ¾ cup

AVOCADO BUTTER

1 small avocado, peeled, stoned and mashed
3 teaspoons lemon juice
125 g unsalted butter
¼ teaspoon ground ginger
2 tablespoons hazelnut meal

Use as a piquant spread in place of butter or chill and slice into pats to serve with grilled fish or green vegetables.

Blend the avocado and lemon juice and beat in the butter and ginger. Shape the mixture into a roll, wrap closely with greaseproof paper and chill until firm. Slice the avocado butter and roll lightly in the hazelnut meal. Omit the nuts if using as a spread.

Makes ¾ cup

CHANTILLY CREAM

1 cup cream, chilled
2 teaspoons sifted icing sugar
2 tablespoons iced water
¼ teaspoon vanilla essence

Use an electric hand beater or blender set on low speed, a food processor is too fast. Put all the ingredients into a mixing bowl and beat until the cream has doubled in volume. Increase the rate of whisking for the last minute or so until the cream is fluffy.

AVOCADO MAYONNAISE

1 egg yolk
½ teaspoon salt
½ teaspoon white pepper
¼ teaspoon dry mustard
pinch castor sugar
2 teaspoons warm water
½ cup olive or vegetable oil
2½ teaspoons white wine vinegar or lemon juice
1 small avocado, peeled, stoned and mashed

Although this mayonnaise does not discolour rapidly it is better when prepared and used on the same day. Serve with eggs, vegetables, cold meat and fish.

Whip the egg yolk, seasoning and water until fluffy. You can use a blender, food processor or whisk. Gradually add the oil, blending until the mixture thickens. Add the vinegar and avocado, blend again until smooth. Cover the surface closely with plastic film or greaseproof paper and chill before serving.

Makes 1 cup

VINAIGRETTE SAUCE

The basic vinaigrette recipe is simple and once mixed can be varied very easily.

Basic Vinaigrette

1 cup olive or safflower oil
3 tablespoons wine vinegar
2 teaspoons lemon juice
salt
black pepper

Shake the oil, vinegar and lemon juice together and season to taste with salt and pepper. Store in a covered jar in the refrigerator.

Makes 1¼ cups

Cream Vinaigrette

Add 2 tablespoons cream

Favourite Dressing

To the basic vinaigrette add
1 clove garlic, crushed
⅛ teaspoon dry mustard
pinch castor sugar

BLENDER MAYONNAISE

2 egg yolks
pinch castor sugar
½ teaspoon dry mustard
2–3 teaspoons lemon juice
1 cup olive or vegetable oil
salt
white pepper

Whisk the egg yolks, sugar and mustard for a few seconds in a blender or food processor. Add 2 teaspoons lemon juice and blend briefly. With the machine running, pour the oil slowly and steadily onto the egg yolks until the mixture begins to thicken, then the oil can be added more quickly. Season to taste with salt, pepper and more lemon juice if liked. The mayonnaise will keep in the refrigerator, closely covered with plastic film for 1 week.

If the mayonnaise curdles or does not thicken, and this can happen if the temperature is wrong or the eggs are not too fresh, pour the mixture out of the blender into a jug. Wash and dry the blender, add 1 egg yolk, whisk until fluffy. Slowly pour the original mixture onto the egg and blend until thick. Adjust seasoning before storing.

Makes 1¼ cups

BLENDER HOLLANDAISE SAUCE

125 g butter, preferably unsalted
2 egg yolks
1½ tablespoons lemon juice
¼ teaspoon salt
¼ teaspoon Tabasco sauce

Melt the butter and leave over moderate heat until hot, do not let it brown. Whisk the remaining ingredients together in a food processor or blender. Pour the hot butter onto the eggs in a slow stream. Turn the machine off when all of the butter has been added. Use the sauce immediately or keep warm over barely simmering water.

Note If the sauce is left until it becomes too thick it can be revived by blending, briefly, with 2–3 teaspoons of hot water.

Makes ¾ cup

Index

Complete list of recipes by sections in alphabetical order.
Bold italic figures indicate illustration page numbers.